"I've Ridden It... and I'm Convinced"

Discriminating Youngsters Unanimously Endorse the Distinctive **NEW** JOHN DEERE TRACTORCYCLE

NEW 70 SERIES 4-WHEEL-DRIVE TRACTORS

THE POWER-PLUS TRACTORS

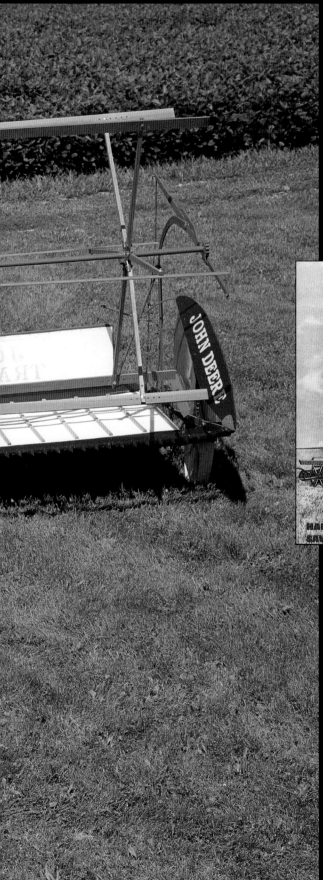

The **JOHN DEERE**
Tractor Legacy

JOHN DEERE
LICENSED PRODUCT

JOHN DEERE
NO.55
Self-Propelled
COMBINE

HARVESTS MORE ACRES EVERY DAY
SAVES MORE GRAIN AT LOWER COST

DEERE & COMPANY
MOLINE, ILL,

Manufacturers of
PLOWS.
SULKY PLOWS AND CULTIVATORS.

Don Macmillan, Editor

Foreword by Charles Velie James

With Wayne G. Broehl Jr., Harold L. Brock,
Ralph W. Sanders, and Orrin E. Miller

Voyageur Press

First published in 2003 by Voyageur Press, an imprint of MBI Publishing Company, 400 1st Avenue North, Suite 300, Minneapolis, MN 55401 USA

The information in this book is true and complete to the best of our knowledge. All recommendations are made without any guarantee on the part of the author or Publisher, who also disclaim any liability incurred in connection with the use of this data or specific details.

We recognize, further, that some words, model names, and designations mentioned herein are the property of the trademark holder. We use them for identification purposes only. This is not an official publication.

Voyageur Press titles are also available at discounts in bulk quantity for industrial or sales-promotional use. For details write to Special Sales Manager at MBI Publishing Company, 400 1st Avenue North, Suite 300, Minneapolis, MN 55401 USA.

To find out more about our books, join us online at www.voyageurpress.com.

Edited by Michael Dregni; Designed by JoDee Mittlestadt
Printed in China

Library of Congress Cataloging-in-Publication Data

The John Deere legacy / Don Macmillan, editor ; foreword by Charles Velie James ; with Wayne G. Broehl Jr.
   p. cm.

ISBN-13: 978-0-7603-4014-1

1. John Deere tractors—History. 2. Deere & Company—History.
I. Macmillan, Don. II. Broehl, Wayne G.
   TL233.6.J64J633 2003
   629.225'2'09—dc21

2003006363

On the frontispiece: *John Deere displays his first self-scouring steel plow in this painting by Walter Haskell Hinton. A tot sits at the wheel of his Eska-built Deere Tractorcycle. 70 Series brochure, 1993. 1937 John Deere Model A. Owners: Phyllis and Wayne Pokorny. (Photograph © Ralph W. Sanders)*

On the title pages: *1936 John Deere Model B and 1935 John Deere Tractor Binder. Owners: Don McKinley and Marvin Huber. (Photograph © Ralph W. Sanders)*

On the contributors page: *An 8300T discs a spring field.*

Contributors

Don Macmillan is one of the world's most respected authorities on Deere & Company. He bought his first Deere tractor in 1943, was appointed the first Deere dealer in the United Kingdom in 1958, and went on to establish one of the world's foremost collections of Deere tractors and memorabilia. Working with Deere & Company, he authored *John Deere Tractors & Equipment* volumes 1 and 2 and *John Deere Tractors Worldwide*, all published by the American Society of Agricultural Engineers. He is also the author of *The Big Book of John Deere Tractors* and *The Field Guide to John Deere Tractors* as well as a contributor to *The Little Book of John Deere* and *This Old John Deere*, all published by Voyageur Press.

Charles Velie James is the great, great grandson of John Deere.

Ralph W. Sanders has photographed and authored three books of farm tractor history—*Ultimate John Deere: The History of the Big Green Machines, Vintage Farm Tractors,* and *Vintage International Harvester Tractors,* all published by Voyageur Press. Ralph has also photographed numerous antique tractor calendars. Ralph's forty-six-year farm-related career includes sixteen years in farm journalism and thirty years in agricultural photography.

Orrin E. Miller worked for Deere as a skilled trades machinist creating dies for tractor parts. After he retired, he began researching Deere and Waterloo, Iowa, history.

Harold L. Brock was a tractor design engineer from 1939 to 1958 for Henry Ford's revolutionary N Series Ford-Ferguson machines before coming to Deere & Company as a New Generation tractor engineering executive from 1959 to 1985. He was the president of the Society of Automotive Engineers in 1971.

Wayne G. Broehl Jr. is the author of *John Deere's Company: A History of Deere & Company and its Times.* He is a historian and faculty member of Dartmouth College's Amos Tuck School of Business Administration.

Acknowledgments

Our thanks first and foremost to those at Deere & Company who helped make this book possible, including, in alphabetical order, Tim Caldwell, Vicki L. Eller, Kasia Finnan, Dean Hamke, and Les Stegh.

Thanks also to Harold L. Brock, Wayne G. Broehl Jr., Charles Velie James, Don Macmillan, Orrin E. Miller, and Ralph W. Sanders.

Finally, a special thanks to Robert N. Pripps for all of his invaluable assistance with this project.

Contents

Foreword

By Charles Velie James

Charles Velie James is the great, great grandson of John Deere.

I am proud and thrilled to have been asked to write the foreword to this new book about the company founded by my great, great grandfather, John Deere. In this regard, I wish to tell you something about his early history and the man himself.

John was born in 1804 in Vermont to William and Sarah Yates Deere, both of English heritage. At age seventeen, young John put aside his schoolbooks to become an apprentice blacksmith in Middlebury, Vermont. In time, he achieved the reputation of a master blacksmith.

Following his marriage to Demarius Lamb, he started his own "smithy," only to see it burn to the ground a few months later. Using what remained of his savings, as fire insurance was relatively unknown in those days, he rebuilt two more times, with the same disastrous result each time. Discouraged and with no savings, he took a job as a blacksmith in a stagecoach and wagon terminal in Royalton, Vermont. It was here that he heard about the lure of the West from the drivers and their passengers. At this point in his life, John also felt that the East was becoming too industrialized, machines now doing the work that man had always done with his hands.

So, in 1836, with $73.73 in his pocket, John traveled to Chicago via the Erie Canal and Great Lakes, and from there by wagon to Grand Detour, Illinois, which at the moment had a great need for a blacksmith, the nearest one being some forty miles away.

To John, Grand Detour and its gently rolling surrounding environment was the land of his dreams, where a plow could upturn the earth for miles, unlike the rocky soil of Vermont. It was here that he built a blacksmith shop and made a home for his family.

However, he soon learned from the other settlers from New England who had preceded him that the wood and iron plows that had worked well in the gravely soil of the East couldn't handle the rich, sticky loam of the West. It was all that horses and oxen could do to draw the plows through this soil, which clung to the plow and had to be repeatedly and exhaustingly shoveled or paddled clear. Word was passed that the immigrant farmers should shun the prairies and either push farther west to timber country, or return east.

Deere was greatly troubled that so many in this beautiful country were giving up over the failure of a single farm implement, the plow. However, if ever this fertile land was to be conquered, it was not by any plow then in existence. John made it his personal challenge to forge a plow that would scour itself with a surface to which soil wouldn't cling. In pondering a solution, he had seen saws made of steel in milling operations and sensed that the shining surface of steel plate might be able to repel the soil. So, in the face of many skeptics and scoffers, he painstakingly and patiently forged the world's first steel plow.

On a summer day in 1838, with a large group of farmers looking on, Deere's horse-drawn steel plow penetrated the ground easily and emerged cleanly from the black earth. By the end of that day, Deere had more orders for steel plows than his "smithy" could deliver in many a day. His plow revolutionized the world of agriculture.

As word of this self-scouring plow spread, the demand became overwhelming. In 1847, Deere moved his growing business from Grand Detour to Moline to gain access to the Mississippi thoroughfare. The rest is history.

In 1868, the company was incorporated under the

A smiling farm boy pilots his Deere tractor in this famous painting by artist Walter Haskell Hinton that graced the cover of a Model A and B tractor brochure.

Above: *Another smiling boy pilots his Deere Tractorcycle.*

Left: *A restored 1940 Model HWH with dual rear wheels. Owner: Doug Pelzer. (Photograph by Hans Halberstadt)*

name Deere & Company. In growing the business, Deere was always intensely loyal to his family and those who married into it, involving them in the business wherever and whenever possible. Thus, in 1863, Stephen Velie, who married Deere's sixth child and fourth daughter, Emma, my great grandmother, joined the business and, following incorporation, became its Secretary and Treasurer, as well as a Director. Stephen and Emma had three sons, all of whom eventually became active in the management and direction of Deere & Company.

To quote from a letter that Stephen Velie wrote to his eldest son, my grandfather, Charles Deere Velie, about his father-in-law and Charles's grandfather, on his eightieth birthday, two years before his death, "John Deere owes his success to hard work, integrity of purpose and a natural faculty of concentrating all his powers on 'one thing at a time.' Whenever he set about doing anything, it seemed to be decided in his mind that that was the right thing to do and now was the time to do it and he went right ahead towards its accomplishment; and his faculty of concentration combined with a broad charity, a lively sympathy with struggling humanity and a sterling integrity has given him the character and made him the reputation he now enjoys."

CHAPTER 1

Roots, 1837–1911

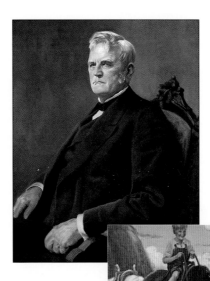

DEERE & CO.,
Sole Manufacturers, Moline, Illinois.

Grant Wood was the quintessential artist of the farmlands and his painting of a plow at rest before a farm vista spoke of John Deere's legacy in agriculture.

John Deere, Blacksmith

John Deere—the man whose name was to become famous around the globe as the world's leading farm-machinery manufacturer—was born in 1804 in Vermont, the son of an English immigrant to the New World. John Deere grew up to be a practical rather than a theoretical man. He apprenticed himself to a Captain Benjamin Lawrence to learn the trade of blacksmith, an apprenticeship he completed in 1825. Setting up his own smithery, John Deere earned a reputation for making hay forks, polishing the lines "until they slipped out of the hay like needles," and his shovels and hoes were "like no others . . . by reason of their smooth and satiny surface." It was an augury for the future.

With times hard in Vermont in 1836, John Deere decided to follow another Vermonter, Leonard Andrus, to Grand Detour on the Rock River in Illinois, about 100 miles (160 km) west of Chicago. Andrus had started a saw-mill, and it was while working for him that John Deere found the broken saw blade that inspired his idea to make the world's first successful steel plow. John Deere's plow was demonstrated and sold to the farmer Lewis Crandall. As word of Deere's plow spread, further orders ensued. Within ten years, John Deere's smithery was crafting 1,000 plows annually.

This success led to a move from Grand Detour to Moline in 1848 due its position on the Mississippi River and its extensive transport facilities. John Deere hired Robert N. Tate to supervise plow manufacture and in 1848, added John Gould to look after the partnership's finances. In the first five months of 1849, Deere made 1,200 plows. By 1857, just twenty years after making his first plow, John Deere's company had produced a total of 13,400 plows of seven types.

"Haying-Time: The Last Load" is a Currier & Ives lithograph depicting the bucolic life of the farmer in the late 1800s.

A farm family proudly poses before its prairie sodhouse in the mid 1800s.

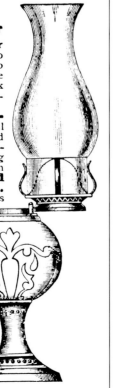

KEROSENE LAMP.
Burner-Collar & Filler

Every person who has ever filled a Kerosene Oil Lamp knows what a disagreeable job it is, mostly because you have no place to put burner and wick without soiling hands and everything else with oil.

Our New Burner-Collar and Filler avoids all this. Simply press a spring and swing burner to one side, without removing chimney, leaving top of lamp clear as shown in cut. **Neat, Simple and does not show on lamp.** As much a part of the lamp as the burner.

Fits any lamp. "A" size for the ordinary house lamp, **10c.** "B" size, for store lamps, **15c. Agents make big money,** one to six sold in every house. One dozen, "A" size, by mail, **75c.;** one dozen "B" size, **85c.**

Address all orders,

J. BRIDE & CO.,
122 NASSAU ST.,
NEW YORK.

NUMBER LI.

THE
FARMER'S ALMANACK,
CALCULATED ON A NEW AND IMPROVED PLAN,
FOR THE YEAR OF OUR LORD
1843;

Being the 3d after Bissextile or Leap Year, and 67th of Am. Independence.

Fitted to the city of Boston, but will answer for the adjoining States.

Containing, besides the large number of Astronomical Calculations, and the Farmer's Calendar for every month in the year, as great a variety as any other Almanack of

NEW, USEFUL, AND ENTERTAINING MATTER.

BY ROBERT B. THOMAS.

TIME never 'bates his usual pace,
Nor stops his steed, for man or place,
But Jehu-like, drives all the world round,
As swift as top by school-boy twirl'd round.

Anon.

BOSTON:
PUBLISHED AND SOLD BY JENKS & PALMER.

Sold, also, by most Booksellers and Traders throughout the New England States.

[Entered, according to act of Congress, in the year 1842, by Charles J. Hendee, in the Clerk's Office of the District Court of Massachusetts.]

The Value of a Good Horse

WINNING THE PEACE

A team of workhorses provides invaluable help to a farmer in breaking the soil.

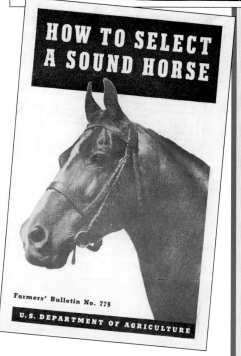

John Deere's Blacksmithery

Above: *John Deere's reconstructed blacksmithery at the John Deere Historic Site. In 1962, University of Illinois archaeologists found the location of the blacksmith shop where John Deere developed his first steel plow in 1837.*

Left: *John Deere and his wife Demarius's home at Grand Detour, Illinois, built in 1836.*

Far left: *The reconstructed forge in John Deere's blacksmithery.*

TIMELINE

1804: John Deere is born February 7, in Rutland, Vermont.

1800s: Small family farms dominate North America.

1807: Robert Fulton travels up the Hudson River on his steamboat, *Clermont,* setting a course for steam power.

1819: Jethro Wood patents his iron plow.

1825: The Erie Canal opens, making water transportation possible from New York City along the Hudson River and through the Great Lakes to the Midwest.

1830: 250–300 labor-hours are required to produce 100 bushels of wheat with a walking plow, brush harrow, hand broadcasting of seed, a hand sickle and flail.

1831: Cyrus Hall McCormick demonstrates his grain reaper near Steele's Tavern in Virginia. International Harvester later blossoms from his invention.

1836: John Deere travels to Grand Detour, Illinois, by way of the Erie Canal, Lake Erie, and Lake Michigan looking for opportunities in the new West.

1837: John Deere develops the self-scouring steel plow at Grand Detour. The city of Chicago, Illinois, incorporates with 4,853 residents. Samuel Morse invents his telegraph.

1838: Heinrich Lanz is born in Germany.

1840: Farmers make up 69 percent of the U.S. labor force. The growing use of factory-built ag machinery increases farmers' need for cash and encourages commercial farming. New York, Pennsylvania, and Ohio are the chief wheat-growing states. Hereford, Ayrshire, Galloway, Jersey, and Holstein cattle are imported and bred.

1841: The grain drill is patented. *Prairie Farmer* magazine starts the spread of practical farming information. John Deere uses the new publication to advertise his products.

1842: Jerome Increase Case perfects his threshing machine, combining elements of a "ground hog" thresher with those of a fanning mill. He begins producing his thresher in Racine, Wisconsin, in 1844, adding steam engines in 1876 to power his threshers. The first grain elevator is built, in Buffalo, New York.

1845–1847: The Potato Famine in Ireland forces more than a million Irish to immigrate to the U.S.

1848: John Deere moves production of his plow to Moline, Illinois.

1849: The California gold rush draws settlers to the West by the hundreds of thousands, eventually spurring the growth of U.S. agriculture.

1850: Railroads connect most of the eastern United States to the Midwest by rail. 75–90 labor-hours are required to produce 100 bushels of corn with a walking plow, harrow, and hand planting.

1851: The sewing machine is invented.

1852: John Deere plow production reaches 4,000 units annually. The first airship is flown, in France.

1859: Oil is discovered in Pennsylvania. Gasoline becomes a byproduct of kerosene, or "coal oil," production. Heinrich Lanz establishes his factory in Mannheim, Germany, building steam engines and threshers.

1860: Number of U.S. farms: 2,044,000. Average acreage: 199. Wisconsin and Illinois are the chief wheat-growing states. Kerosene lamps become popular.

1861: Abraham Lincoln is inaugurated as the 16th U.S. president. The Civil War begins. Horses and mules start to replace oxen as the farmer's prime mover.

1863: John Deere builds the Hawkeye Sulky cultivator, its first implement with a seat for the operator. It increases the acres of corn that a grower can cultivate.

1865: Abraham Lincoln is assassinated just as the Civil War is ending.

Building Deere Plows:
From Blacksmithery to Factory

In July 1864, the company was reconstituted as Deere & Company with John Deere and son Charles as equal partners. John Deere's various partnerships finally ended in 1868 when the company was incorporated. In its first full year of trading, Deere & Company sold 41,133 plows, cultivators, and harrows with a turnover of $646,563.

Above: *At work within John Deere's blacksmithery.*

Top left: *A farmer walks behind a single-bottom Deere plow pulled by his trusty horse team.*

Top right: *John Deere's son Charles served as Deere & Company president from 1886 to his death on October 29, 1907.*

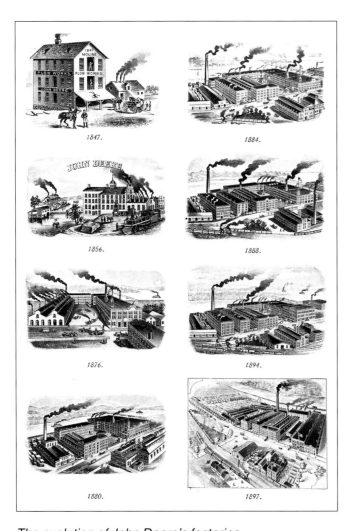

The evolution of John Deere's factories.

Building the U.S. Capitol in Washington, D. C., 1860.

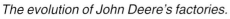

The railroad reaches across the North American continent in 1869.

Building Deere Plows:
From Blacksmithery to Factory

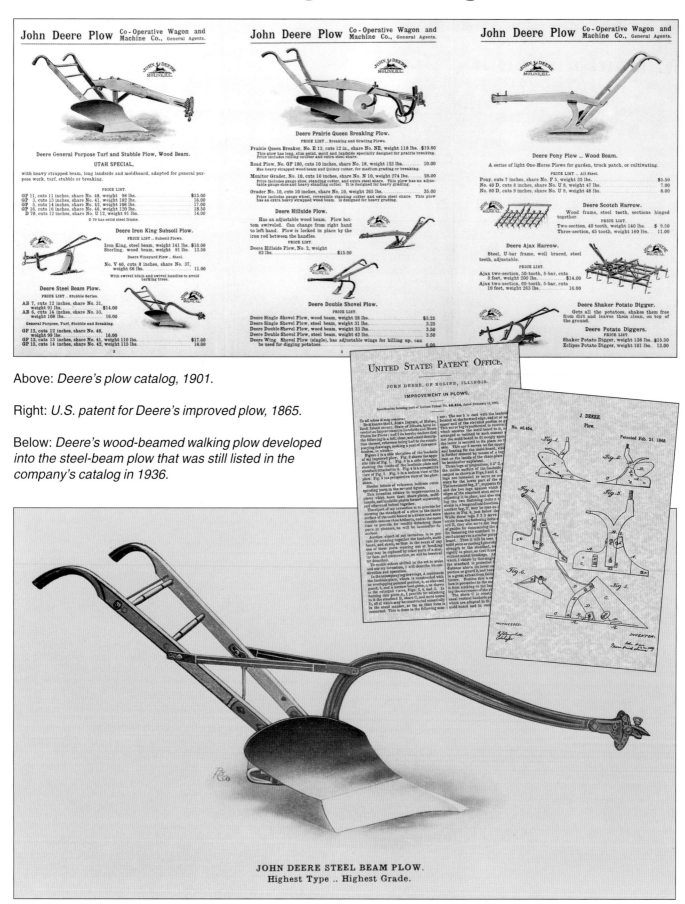

Above: *Deere's plow catalog, 1901.*

Right: *U.S. patent for Deere's improved plow, 1865.*

Below: *Deere's wood-beamed walking plow developed into the steel-beam plow that was still listed in the company's catalog in 1936.*

JOHN DEERE STEEL BEAM PLOW.
Highest Type .. Highest Grade.

Alvah Mansur formed Deere, Mansur & Company, Deere's first independent branch house, located in Kansas City.

A railcar loaded with Deere plows, 1882.

The Farmer's Innovator: From Walking Plows to Sulky Plows

The firm was becoming recognized as an innovator in the field. In 1863, the company's catalog included the Hawkeye Sulky cultivator, Deere's first break from plow making and its first ride-on machine. In 1874, Deere introduced its first gang plows with double- or triple-bottoms. The following year brought the introduction of Gilpin Moore's patented sulky plow, which became so well known that it fundamentally influenced the growth of the company. It won so many firsts in competition that Charles Deere decided to enter it in the famous Paris Exhibition of 1878 where it again easily won and was presented with a special prize of a Sevres vase. It was a major boost for the company and acknowledgment of the firm's two most famous products, the Gilpin sulky and Deere gang plow.

In 1876, the Hawkeye cultivator was replaced by the Peerless & Deere riding models. A forty-tine Scotch harrow was added to the line. Deere & Mansur introduced a corn planter in 1877 and a cornstalk cutter in 1879.

A major improvement for the Gilpin in 1881 was a power-lift, allowing the company to claim it was "The King of the Riding Plows." In 1884, its gang plows adopted a three-wheel configuration and the name New Deal Gangs; by 1889, all the firm's three-wheel plows were called New Deal. Deere entered the haymaking field in 1885 with its sulky rake.

On May 17, 1886, John Deere died at age 82. He had a knack for organization and an abiding concern for quality that has persisted to today in his company.

Above: *John Deere looms above the Moline Plow Works on this 1882 catalog.*

Right: *An advertising postcard for Deere's light draft plows.*

THE NEW DEERE
FOR THE NEW YEAR

The way to make your Corn Planter business pay best is to follow the Good Old Saint's example. In other words, take the

NEW DEERE NO. 9 PLANTER.

Become a Deere dealer, join the vast army of men who sell Deere Goods and

"Make Money Making Sales."

WRITE FOR PARTICULARS, TERMS, ETC.

DEERE & MANSUR CO.
MOLINE   ILLS.

Deere workers build plows, 1900.

Farm Life from Sunup to Sundown

Farming magazines began to appear in the 1840s offering advice and entertainment to families on the far-off farms.

AMERICAN AGRICULTURIST

FOR THE
Farm, Garden, and Household.

"AGRICULTURE IS THE MOST HEALTHFUL, MOST USEFUL, AND MOST NOBLE EMPLOYMENT OF MAN."—WASHINGTON.

ORANGE JUDD COMPANY, PUBLISHERS AND PROPRIETORS.
Office, 245 BROADWAY.

ESTABLISHED IN 1842.
Published also in German at $1.50 a Year.

$1.50 PER ANNUM, IN ADVANCE.
SINGLE NUMBER, 15 CENTS.
4 Copies for $5; 10 for $12; 20 or more, $1 each.

Entered according to Act of Congress, in February, 1874, by the ORANGE JUDD COMPANY, at the Office of the Librarian of Congress, at Washington.

VOLUME XXXIII.—No. 3.   NEW YORK, MARCH, 1874.   NEW SERIES—No. 326.

PLOWING SOD. — Drawn and Engraved for the American Agriculturist.

The manurial value of a sod plowed beneath the surface very much depends upon the manner in which it is turned under. If the furrow is turned in a continuous strip unbroken and made to lap upon the preceding furrow, as it appears in the above engraving, the utmost value of the sod is secured. For it is only as it becomes decomposed and furnishes food for the succeeding crop that it is of any value. If the furrow is irregularly turned and broken into fragments a large portion of the sod is unburied; it simply dries upon the surface and remains useless. Besides a furrow so turned furnishes a poor seed-bed because it is not compact and solid. On the contrary, a properly turned sod forms an excellent seed-bed. The surface of the field when plowed forms a succession of ridges of soil exactly parallel with each other. When these ridges are harrowed down the sod beneath is not torn up, but is evenly covered with a fine layer of soil just sufficient in depth to form a seed-bed, beneath which there is stored every particle of the sod in the best condition to furnish food for the young plants, the roots of which penetrate the soil exactly where their food lies. This is apparent when the position of the furrow slices, as above shown, is observed.

Unfortunately we possess few plows that are capable of turning such a furrow as is here described. The mold-boards of our plows are in general too short to turn a perfectly unbroken furrow. The better farming of our neighbors, the Canadians, and the English farmers, is to some extent due to the extreme care with which they plow, especially sod land. With us the yield of corn depends greatly upon the manner in which the sod is plowed, and the kind of plow we use becomes a very important consideration. The plow shown in the engraving is an iron beam English one, of the Scotch pattern, having a share about four feet long. Its great length enables it to turn the furrows with perfect regularity, leaving the soil in the best condition.

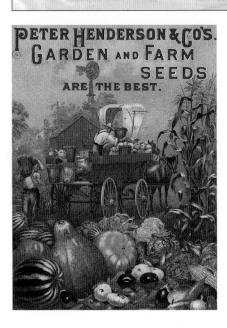

MADAME DEAN'S SPINAL SUPPORTING CORSETS.

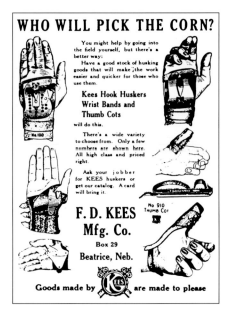

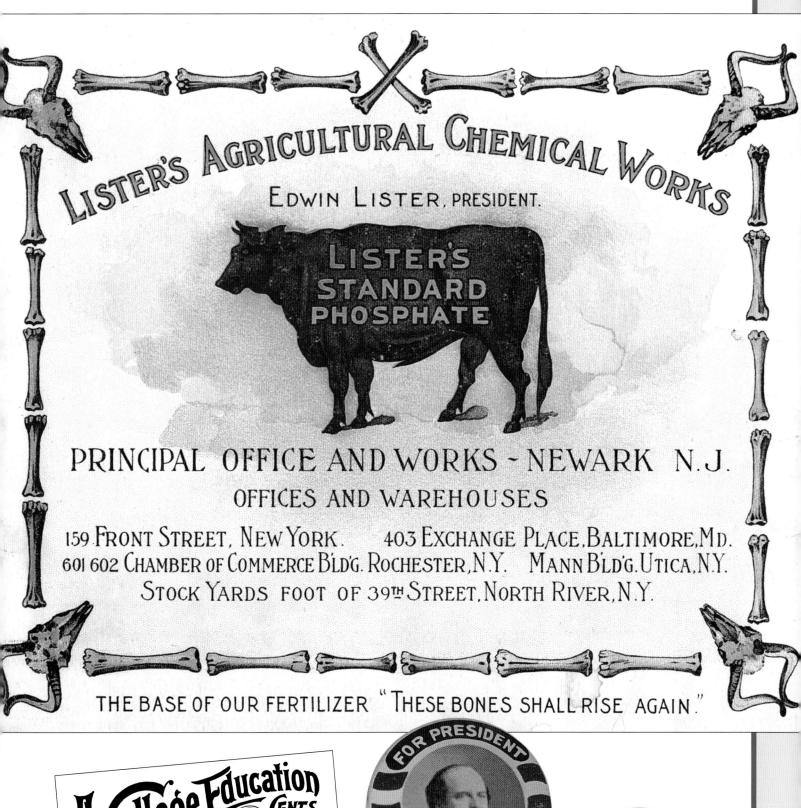

LISTER'S AGRICULTURAL CHEMICAL WORKS

EDWIN LISTER, PRESIDENT.

LISTER'S STANDARD PHOSPHATE

PRINCIPAL OFFICE AND WORKS - NEWARK N.J.

OFFICES AND WAREHOUSES

159 FRONT STREET, NEW YORK.   403 EXCHANGE PLACE, BALTIMORE, MD.
601 602 CHAMBER OF COMMERCE BLD'G. ROCHESTER, N.Y.   MANN BLD'G. UTICA, N.Y.
STOCK YARDS FOOT OF 39TH STREET, NORTH RIVER, N.Y.

THE BASE OF OUR FERTILIZER "THESE BONES SHALL RISE AGAIN."

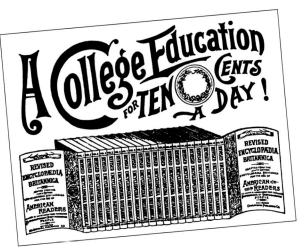

The Development of Farm Power

Left: *Early horse powers like this Fearless used a treadmill to power threshing machines via a leather belt drive.*

Below: *As threshing machines grew in size, many large farmers put their horses to pasture and replaced them with a powerful, expensive steam engine.*

The Dingee Woodbury Power.

Above: *The sweep horse power such as this Dingee Woodbury of the 1890s featured six horse teams hitched to the wheel-drawn circular unit. The power was transmitted to a threshing machine by a tumbling rod. This sweep design was the final, most advanced version.*

Top: *Steam engines required large crews—and a large cash outlay. For smaller farmers—or those who distrusted the Steam Revolution—hay-powered horses continued to power their farms.*

TIMELINE

1868: On August 15, 1868, Deere & Company is incorporated with a capitalization of $150,000. John Deere is president and his son, Charles Deere, vice-president. That year the company sells 41,000 implements.

1869: The Transcontinental railroad is joined at Promontory Point, Utah. Campbell's canned soup is introduced.

1870: Corn becomes the dominant crop in the Midwest. Silos come into use.

1875: John Deere's Gilpin Sulky Plow is designed by Gilpin Moore with a seat for the operator.

1876: Alexander Graham Bell invents the telephone.

1876: Germany's Nicolaus Otto patents his four-stroke internal-combustion engine.

1877: Charles Deere and Alvah Mansur start Deere & Mansur to build corn planters. Thomas Edison introduces his phonograph. His light bulb debuts in 1879, and by 1892, he has an electric-generating station in New York City. The Statue of Liberty is erected.

1880s: Steam traction engines are used on farms not only to power machines but to till the soil with gang plows.

1885: Germany's Karl Benz builds a three-wheeled automobile.

1886: John Deere dies on May 17, 1886, at the age of eighty-two.

On the Road to Becoming a Full-Line Company

During the first twenty-five years of the company's development, the firm concentrated on tillage equipment, but over the next twenty-five years it took the necessary steps to become a full-line company.

In 1907, just before the death of Charles Deere, Deere & Company acquired the Fort Smith Wagon Company. The same year John Deere Plow Company Limited was formed in Canada, the company's major export market. In 1908, Deere set up an export office in New York City as the John Deere Export Company at 17 Battery Place. However, in 1911, it was decided to move back to Moline and the Export Department was set up there on April 1, 1912.

Over the first ten years of the new century, Deere joined forces or acquired compatible companies with different farm machinery lines. Early in 1911, seven companies joined the new Deere family, including Deere & Mansur Company with its corn planters; Syracuse Chilled Plow Company with specialized plows for Eastern soil conditions; Dain Manufacturing Company's hay tools;

Moline Wagon Company with its wagon line; Kemp & Burpee's manure spreaders; Van Brunt Manufcturing Company grain drills; and Marseilles Company with its force-feed automatic corn shellers and grain elevators. These extra manufacturing facilities, plus twenty-two sales organizations, gave Deere & Company a full line of implements and a nationwide distribution system. The merger benefited the manufacturing companies and their customers who could now purchase all their farm machinery requirements from a single John Deere dealership.

Dain Manufacturing Company and its line of hay-making equipment was purchased by Deere in 1910, and Joseph Dain became a Deere vice president and board member.

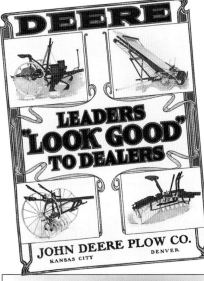

Deere got into the wagon-making business when it purchased the Moline Wagon Company and the Davenport Wagon Company in 1910.

Above: *Deere Secretary Stephen Velie steered the company on a cautious and conservative course.*

Below: *Deere's extensive Moline Plow Works, 1890s.*

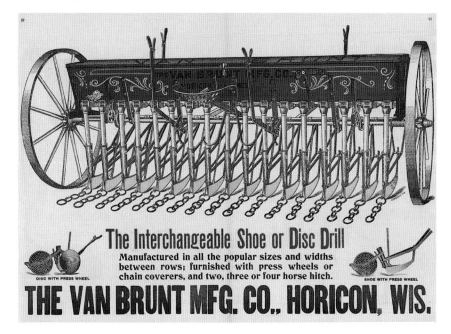

Deere purchased the Van Brunt Manufacturing Company of Horicon, Wisconsin, in 1911, extending its line of farm implements with Van Brunt's drills.

On the Road to Becoming a Full-Line Company

Above: *The farmboy's first lesson—behind a Deere plow, of course.*

Left: *Deere paperweight, 1900.*

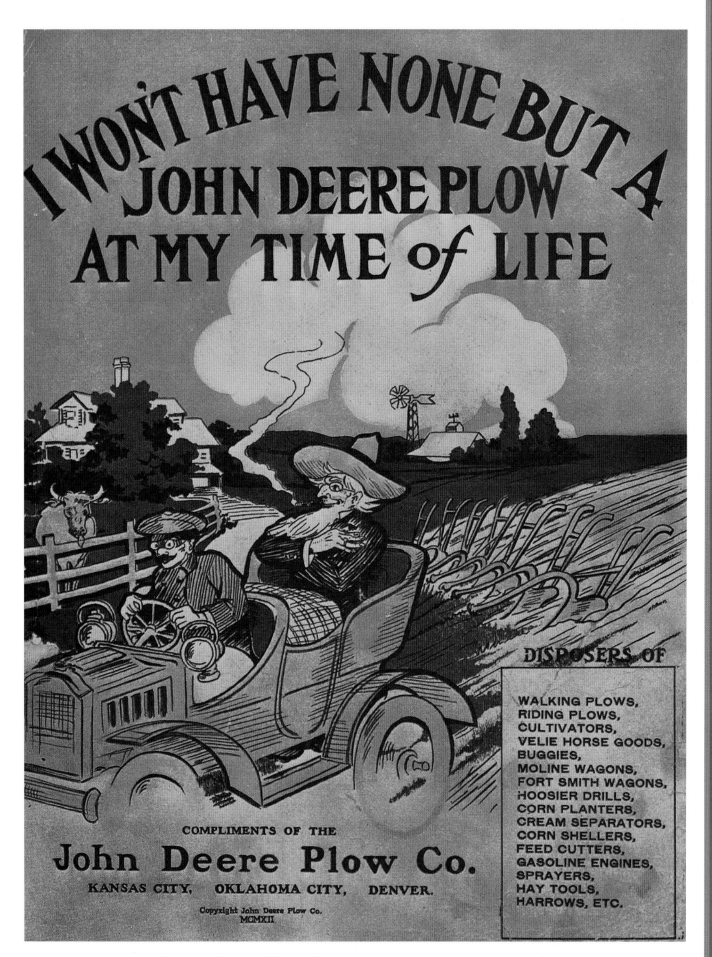

A farmer made wealthy by using Deere's Gilpin sulky plow extols the implement's virtues while plowing fields complete with a chauffeur.

WATERLOO BOY TR

BURNS KEROSENE COMPLET

Points of Merit

1. **Simple Design**—easy to understand—you can expert it yourself.
2. **Burns Kerosene.** Patented manifold gasifies the kerosene and saves many dollars in fuel cost every year. No kerosene to work past piston rings into crank case to destroy quality of lubricating oil and result in burning out bearings.
3. **Powerful Two-Cylinder Engine** delivers its full rated 25 horse-power on belt and 12 horse-power on draw-bar.
4. **Heavy Two-Throw Balanced Crank Shaft**—long-lived motor and increased power due to lack of vibration.
5. **Simple and Positive Oiling System**—automatic—extremely low oil consumption.
6. **Water Cooled** by large core radiator. Capacity of cooling system, 13 gallons. Water circulated by reliable centrifugal pump.
7. **Reliable Ignition**—simple high tension magneto with impulse starter.
8. **Extra Strong Gears,** case-hardened, heat-treated, dust-proof, run in oil.
9. **Roller Bearings** at all important points reduce friction and conserve power.
10. **Right-Hand Drive Wheel in Furrow**—a big advantage in plowing—prevents side draft on plow and tractor. Self-steering.
11. **Pulley Driven Direct** from engine crank shaft—a big advantage in belt work—no gears in mesh—every ounce of power utilized.
12. **Low Repair Cost** and John Deere repair service.

Pulling a John Deere 3-bottom plow. Drive wheel in furrow—no plow or tractor side draft.

Pulling John Deere Heavy Tractor Disc Harrow and Brillion Pulverizer—good seed beds rapidly.

Pulling two John Deere 8-foot binders— harvesting done at the right tim

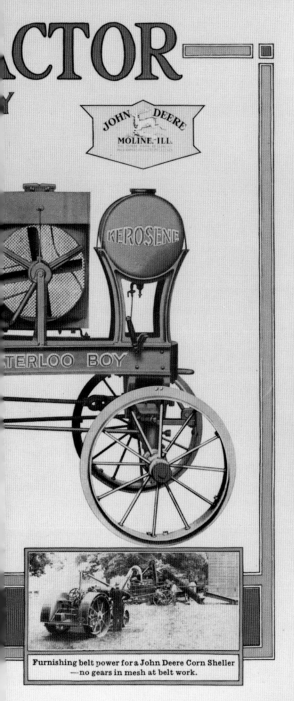

Furnishing belt power for a John Deere Corn Sheller
—no gears in mesh at belt work.

CHAPTER 2

Pioneering Farm Tractors, 1892–1922

Deere's Waterloo Boy became the firm's first farm tractor to go into large-scale production.

The Road to Power Farming

The first tractor to propel itself both forward and backward was designed by thresherman and inventor John Froelich in 1892. Froelich's creation was the predecessor of the tractors built by the Waterloo Gasoline Engine Company. The firm built an array of tractors and stationary engines that were christened with the name "Waterloo Boy."

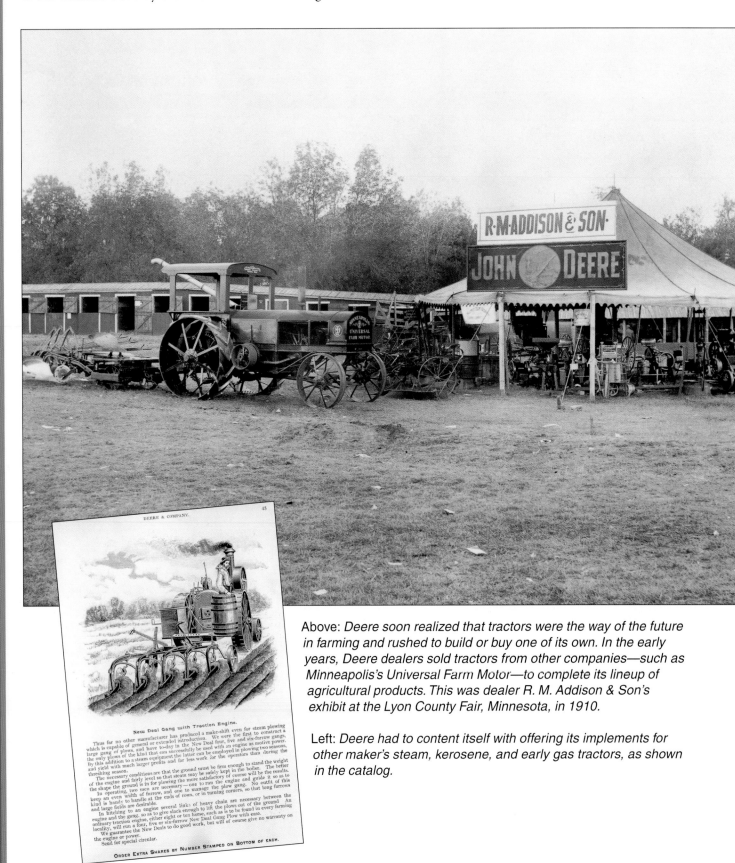

Above: *Deere soon realized that tractors were the way of the future in farming and rushed to build or buy one of its own. In the early years, Deere dealers sold tractors from other companies—such as Minneapolis's Universal Farm Motor—to complete its lineup of agricultural products. This was dealer R. M. Addison & Son's exhibit at the Lyon County Fair, Minnesota, in 1910.*

Left: *Deere had to content itself with offering its implements for other maker's steam, kerosene, and early gas tractors, as shown in the catalog.*

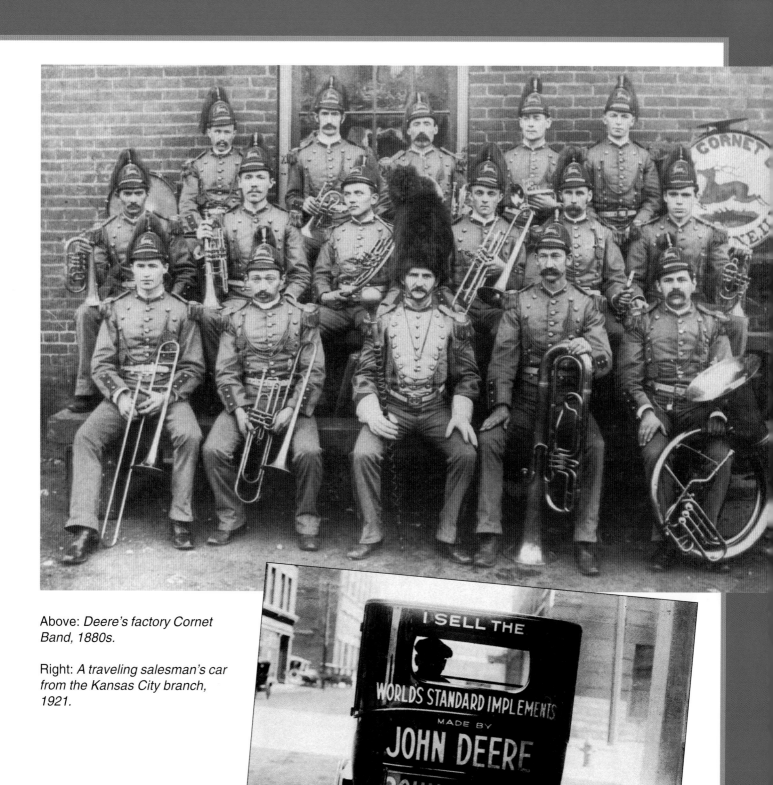

Above: *Deere's factory Cornet Band, 1880s.*

Right: *A traveling salesman's car from the Kansas City branch, 1921.*

The Road to Power Farming

Farmer's-son-turned-inventor Henry Ford launched his Ford Model T automobile in 1908 with a gas-powered internal-combustion engine. Ford never forgot his farming roots and worked to build an inexpensive, lightweight tractor based on the same concepts as his Model T.

Above: *Power farming was a new term in the turn of the century.*

Right: *Upon the death of Charles Deere, his son-in-law William Butterworth became president of Deere & Company. Butterworth served as president from 1907 to 1928 and chairman from 1928 to 1936.*

THE FUTURE OF THE AIRSHIP IN AGRICULTURE

Anything seemed possible with the revolution in technology following the turn of the century. This cartoon may have been half satire, half wishful thinking, but either way, the cartoonist certainly saw the farm tractor as having a short future given the recent advances in dirigibles.

JOHN FROELICH.

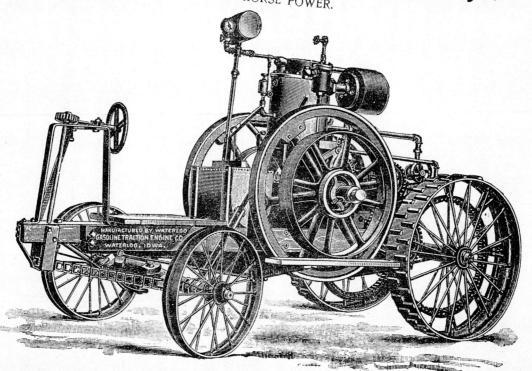

Waterloo Gasoline Traction Engine.

16-HORSE POWER.

John Froelich:
The Story of a Man and a Tractor

By Orrin E. Miller

The word "froelich" means joyous, merry, happy, and in good spirits in German. Inventor John Froelich's father Henry was born in 1813 in Kassel, Grand Ducy of Hesse, Germany. He came to America in the early 1840s, landing in Dubuque, Iowa. He then worked his way north and came to the home of Herman Schneider, whom he had known in Germany. Henry fell in love with the countryside, and soon invested in land, purchased for $1.25 per acre from the U.S. government. This property was just west of the future village. The Froelich farm today is marked by a grove of German white pine and European larch, which originally numbered about 680 trees. The seeds for these trees were brought from Germany on a later, 1870s trip to his homeland. After an 1846 trip to Germany, he returned to McGregor's landing on June 6, 1847, with a group of twenty-eight fellow immigrants. One of the people in the returning group was a Kathryn Gutheil, who would later become Henry's wife.

By 1870, everyone was anxiously waiting the coming of the railroad, triggering the building of the village of Froelich. Where the tracks crossed over the state road, the first businesses and houses were built. The town got its name from Henry, who was the first postmaster at Froelich, then known as Froelich Station.

John was their first child, born on November 24, 1849. In 1851, Fred was born, followed by Ben, Martha, Etta, and Edwin. As he grew, John's education was simple. He attended an academy in Galena, Illinois, but this contributed nothing of a mechanical nature. His knowledge was almost entirely intuitive, and he learned from his mistakes.

John Froelich built a grain elevator near Beulah Junction on the narrow-gauge side of the railroad tracks that ran from Froelich to Beulah. He then devised a way of lifting the smaller, narrow-gauge grain cars, so the grain would run into the mainline cars. This is the first known use of his inventive genius. The second was in 1883, when he devised a way to move the elevator without disassembly from Beulah to Froelich on railroad flat cars. This was quite a feat in its day, performed on a Sunday when other trains did not run. The elevator was set upright on the flat car and men walked along holding ropes to keep it from falling over. The Chicago, Milwaukee, & St. Paul Rail Road supplied the locomotive but accepted no responsibility in case there was an accident. There were no accidents.

After the elevator was moved in 1883, John developed a mechanical corn picker with an acquaintance, William Mann. After the corn picker was tried out in a nearby field, it was brought back for adjustments and parked inside the elevator. That evening, a hot box in the elevator ignited, setting fire to the building. The elevator burned to the ground along with Froelich's new invention.

A new and larger elevator and mill were built on the foundation of the first elevator. This second elevator burnt to the ground in 1898. It was in the shop of the second elevator and mill that John and William Mann put together the famous Froelich traction engine.

John did threshing locally with a straw-burning steam engine. He purchased the straw burner in 1888 from Waterloo implement dealer S. G. Steward. Because John threshed a lot in South Dakota where wood and coal were

John Froelich's gasoline tractor was not the first gas-powered tractor, but it was the first to combine a solid, working engine with forward and reverse gears, making it a useable and reliable machine.

scarce, he had to rely on straw as a fuel. Aside from the fuel problem, the alkaline prairie water caused scale to form in the steam engine's boiler. John's solution was to develop a gas traction engine.

In 1890, John bought a 4½-hp horizontal stationary gas engine made by John Charter's Charter Gas Engine Company of Sterling, Illinois. He mounted the engine on a well-drilling outfit. The Charter firm had built six gas-powered tractors in 1889 for use by Dakota farmers in threshing. These Charter machines had only a forward gear and no reverse. John Froelich traveled to the Dakotas for threshing work and could have seen or heard about these tractors, if he did not already know about them from doing business with the Charter Company in 1890. John now decided to try using a gas engine as a power source in threshing. The experience gained from installing the Charter engine on his well-drilling outfit led to the development of his first gas tractor with forward and reverse gears.

In building his gas traction engine, John used a stationary engine made by the Van Duzen Company of Cincinnati, Ohio. John visited their plant before purchasing his engine, and the firm became sufficiently interested in his experiment to furnish a factory expert when operating difficulties later manifested themselves. Van Duzen offered in 1894 a traction engine similar to Froelich's, although it was not successful. The Huber company bought out Van Duzen and marketed a traction engine in 1898, the first successful gas traction engine ever offered.

John's Van Duzen engine was a single-cylinder vertical with 14x14-inch (350x350-mm) bore and stroke. He mounted it on a chassis made of two beams of laminated oak, each beam comprised of four or five 2x12-inch planks. These beams were laminated so they would bend together at the front over the front axle pivot, while at the rear they were spread out practically to the driving wheels and parallel to each other.

Many accounts state that a Robinson steam engine frame formed the basis for John's tractor, but this was not true. John did use gears and pulleys purchased from Robinson in the open transmission, however. I believe that he used or copied the Rumely steam engine transmission because Rumely was the only steam engine manufacturer to use a reverse gear; everyone else reversed the engine to back up.

Just how the power was delivered to the rear wheels is not clear; however, a friction drive like that commonly used to drive thresher cylinders was utilized. This consisted of a compressed friction wheel on the powershaft of the engine that engaged a plain iron pulley on a driven shaft. The tractor mechanism differed from the thresher mechanism in that a spring held the mechanism out of engagement, and to start the machine as a tractor, the operator at the steering wheel rode with one foot on the end of a long lever that forced the friction wheels together. All he had to do when he noticed that the engine was slowing down because of too much load was to ease off a little with his foot and let the friction drive slip until the engine picked up speed again. To back up the tractor, a gear was shifted.

The ignition of the Van Duzen engine was not by electric spark plug but rather by a "hot tube." With only ordinary water pipe to make these tubes from, they often blew out and the engine would stop until a new tube could be applied and heated. A carburetor had not yet even been conceived. Fuel was injected into the inflowing air in measured quantities by means of a variable-stroke gasoline pump, which could be easily regulated but of which the valves constantly wore out. Gasoline was then still a by-product of kerosene manufacture and was not uniform in quantity. Still, it was cheap, even in the Dakotas.

A cooling radiator for the jacket water was still unknown; with stationary engines, the jacket was just connected up with the water supply and the water wasted. With a portable machine for use in the field, this would not work. A large rectangular tank carried the cooling water. The water was pumped by an engine-driven pump from the bottom of the tank through the water jacket of the engine and returned to the tank through a wide, shallow trough and a series of baffles, the water being cooled by its contact with the air and by evaporation. This required some water replenishment, but only a barrel or so per day.

In the morning when starting up, the hot tube was heated while the rest of the crew oiled the thresher, put on the belt, and got ready to start threshing. The starting of the engine required several men at the flywheels to pull them over, much as people started airplanes years later. Sufficient gasoline for one explosion was put into the cylinder through an open-top oil cup in the head of the engine. The men then swung hard on the flywheels, rotating them backward, forcing the gas mixture into the hot tube, and igniting the charge before the engine had reached top dead-center. If the gas mixture and swing were just right, the engine upon ignition would turn in the right direction and would have energy enough to get at least another charge into the engine and ignite it, and the engine would be running. If either one or the other was not right, they had to try again.

The starting of the thresher after the engine was running required a belt pulley with a friction clutch, which was mounted on the end of the crankshaft. This clutch had to be operated carefully in order to obtain just enough power to start the thresher and not take so much power

The Froelich tractor in action, working in a South Dakota field in September 1892.

Right: *The original Froelich tractor brochure.*

Below: *A 1/16-scale model of the Froelich tractor made by Scale Models.*

The Only Gasoline Traction Engine
···ON EARTH.···

The **Waterloo**

Gasoline

Traction

Engine.

····MANUFACTURED BY····

The Waterloo Gasoline Traction Engine Co.,
WATERLOO, IOWA, U. S. A.

that it would stop it. This was a somewhat awkward operation to perform. One stood alongside the engine and pushed in or out on a sliding collar.

When traveling, John and his threshing crew lived out of two portable trailers, one a dining room and the other a bunkhouse. Everything was loaded on railroad flat cars and transported to South Dakota. In 1892, John was using a J. I. Case thresher powered by his own traction engine, doing custom threshing around Milbank, Mitchell, and Langford.

When John returned from South Dakota, dealer S. G. Steward of Waterloo either heard about or was contacted concerning John's gas traction engine. Steward and others became interested and persuaded John to bring his invention to Waterloo. A demonstration was held in Waterloo in December 1892, and negotiations followed. A tractor company was formed in the next thirty days. On January 10, 1893, the Waterloo Gasoline Traction Engine Company was organized for the main purpose of manufacturing the Froelich traction engine.

The company was first located in the old Cascaden Foundry on Cedar Street on the west bank of the Cedar River. The Van Duzen gas engine was taken from the first tractor and used as the power source for the newly established company. The Waterloo Gasoline Traction Engine Company remained at this site until about 1900 when it moved across the street. No known pictures exist of this first factory.

Because the fledgling firm sold just two tractors in 1893, another product was needed. Froelich's experience with operating the Charter gas engine led the company to manufacture stationary gas engines. The first stationary engine manufactured locally was installed in the Waterloo *Courier* press room in February 1894, and it worked perfectly for years until replaced by a larger one from the same company.

The Waterloo Gasoline Traction Engine Company ran into financial problems during the nationwide depression of the early 1890s and was forced to reorganize on November 10, 1895, at which time it was renamed the Waterloo Gasoline Engine Company. A patent was issued to John Froelich on his tractor that same month when it is believed he left Waterloo. John's savings and everything he had possessed at the company's beginning—his home, elevator, and a stockyards—were put into the company, and with the firm's failure, all was lost.

While the company reformed without him and went on to develop its Waterloo Boy engines and tractors, John moved on to Marshalltown, Iowa, and eventually to St. Paul, Minnesota. Here, he become a wealthy man due to the development of the Froelich Neostyle Washer, a clothes-washing machine. He died on May 24, 1933, at the age of eighty-four.

Timeline

1892: John Froelich builds the world's first successful gas tractor with forward and reverse gears. Germany's Rudolf Diesel patents his diesel engine.

1893: Henry Ford builds his own car while working at the Edison Illumination Company of Detroit, Michigan.

1896: Rural Free Delivery of mail debuts. Klondike Gold Rush begins.

1897: Jell-O is introduced.

1898: The Spanish-American War starts.

1900: Farmers make up 38 percent of the U.S. labor force with farms averaging 147 acres. Extensive experimental work is carried out to breed disease-resistant and high-yielding plant hybrids. Max Planck formulates his Quantum Theory and Sigmund Freud publishes *The Interpretation of Dreams*. Kodak introduces the $1 Brownie camera. Farm families get their first party line telephones.

1901: President McKinley is assasinated. Vice-President Teddy Roosevelt succeeds him. Radio signals span the Atlantic Ocean. The electric clothes-washing machine is invented.

1902: Hart-Parr in Charles City, Iowa, builds its first gas tractor. The firm later coins the term "tractor." Heinrich Lanz meets Charles Deere, who inspires him and his son, Karl Lanz, to expand production and mechanization. The Teddy Bear debuts.

1903: Wilbur and Orville Wright launch their powered "heavier-than-air" flying machine at Kitty Hawk, North Carolina. The pioneering "motion picture," *The Great Train Robbery*, debuts.

1906: The first plastic, called Bakelite, debuts. Kellogg's Corn Flakes is introduced.

1907: With the death of Charles Deere, William Butterworth succeeds him as company president.

1908: The Ford Motor Company launches the Model T in 1908. Roosevelt's Country Life Commission focuses attention on the problems of farm wives and the difficulty of keeping children on the farm. William Hoover introduces the vacuum cleaner.

1910: Farmers make up 31 percent of the U.S. labor force with farms averaging 138 acres. North Dakota, Kansas, and Minnesota are the chief wheat-growing states. The Panama Canal opens.

1911: The first Farm Bureau is formed. Lanz starts buildings its first tractor, the Landbaumotor.

The Birth of the Waterloo Boy

In 1911, the Waterloo Boy company began tractor production, starting with two four-cylinder truss-frame models: the two-wheel-drive, 25-hp Standard; and a crawler-tracked version in 1912 known as the "Sure Grip, Never Slip."

The following year several different models were tried. The all-wheel-drive C and two-wheel-drive L and LA all featured two-cylinder horizontally opposed engines. But for 1914 the first style of the famous Model R was announced with twin side-by-side cylinders. More than 8,000 of these tractors in twelve different styles using only a single forward and single reverse gear were built until 1917, when a second forward gear was provided to become the Model N.

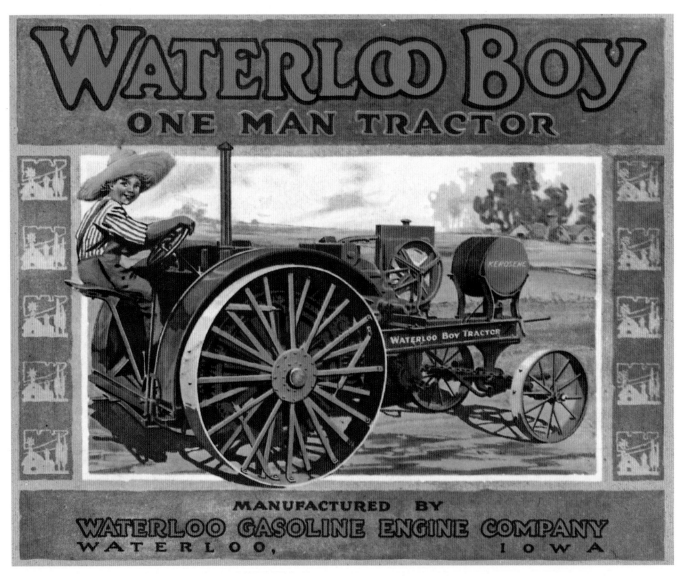

Above: *A Waterloo Boy advertising brochure for the new Model R.*

Right: *The Waterloo Boy Model R of 1916 was rated at 12/24 hp.*

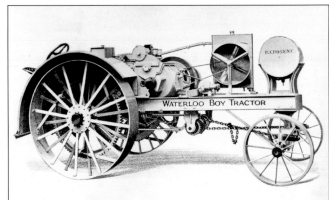

This one-cylinder prototype of the Waterloo Boy was built in 1899 and may have been based on Froelich's gas tractor.

WATERLOO CATAPILLAR
MFG: BY
Waterloo Gasoline Engine Co.
Waterloo, Iowa

Above: *The Waterloo "Catapillar" of 1913 rode on half-tracks and was rated at 12/30 hp.*

Right: *An early, 1914 Waterloo Boy with the firm's first two-cylinder engine.*

Louis W. Witry:

The Man Behind the Waterloo Boy

By Orrin E. Miller

Louis Witry was born in Waterloo, Iowa, in 1870 and spent his entire life in the city. His parents were Dominic and Margaret (Pott) Witry, both of whom were natives of Germany. Dominic Witry was born in 1841 and came to Waterloo in 1868. He entered the employment of Henry Daniels in Waterloo's only sawmill, enabling Dominic to get into the manufacture of furniture. In Germany, Dominic was a cabinet maker by trade. Dominic Witry and Margaret Pott married in Waterloo and had three children: Louis W., Perrie J., and Mary.

Louis was educated in Our Lady of Victory Sisters School in Waterloo. At the age of fifteen, he went to work with the Illinois Central Railroad, where he completed a five-year apprenticeship in the machinist trade. He was then engaged in locomotive work for twelve years, which included traveling throughout the Midwest and out to the West Coast, gaining mechanical experience. In August 1897, he left the Illinois Central Rail Road and started working for the Waterloo Gasoline Engine Company.

When inventor John Froelich left Waterloo in late 1895, there was no one of great mechanical expertise with the Waterloo Gasoline Engine Company for one and a half years until Louis joined the firm and its twenty-person staff. In January 1898, Louis was promoted to factory superintendent and soon after became a stockholder, vice president, and factory manager. This sounds more impressive than it really was, as he still did everything from oiling the machines to sweeping floors when needed. Louis was credited with re-designing the gasoline engines, which improved their product over anything previously produced. This is the main reason employment jumped from twenty men in 1897 to 700 workers by 1914. Under Louis's direction, the Waterloo Gasoline Engine Company flourished.

The Waterloo Boy tractor began as a prototype kerosene tractor called the Big Chief being developed by the Associated Manufacturing Company of Waterloo. Associated Manufacturing was famed for its cream separator sold through Sears, Roebuck mail-order catalogs. The firm started work on its Big Chief but ran into financial trouble, so sold off its Waterloo foundry to the Waterloo Gasoline Company along with the tractor in fall 1911, according to Waterloo courthouse records. The un-marketable Big Chief was then turned over to Louis to tinker with.

Louis lived at 303 Lafayette Street, where he did the so-called research and development of the Waterloo Boy tractor in a backyard shed. The first of Louis's Big Chief developments had an open cooling system that resembled a dog house on the front of the machine. This tractor is credited with 12 hp at the rear wheels and 24 hp off the belt pulley mounted on an extension of the crankshaft at 750 rpm. The two-cylinder horizontal engine started on gasoline and ran on kerosene, as kerosene was cheaper and more plentiful. The fuel was gravity fed with water injection on heavy loads.

Other features of this first tractor were the high-tension magneto with impulse starter, band clutch operated by a hand lever, and the final drive consisting of a large bull gear on the rear wheel driven by a pinion gear. There was one speed forward and one reverse, just like Froelich's first tractor.

Witry's development of the Big Chief, re-named the Waterloo Boy, was first launched on the market in 1912.

After Deere & Company purchased the Waterloo Gasoline Engine Company in March 1918, Louis remained as factory superintendent.

Waterloo Boy advertisement, 1918.

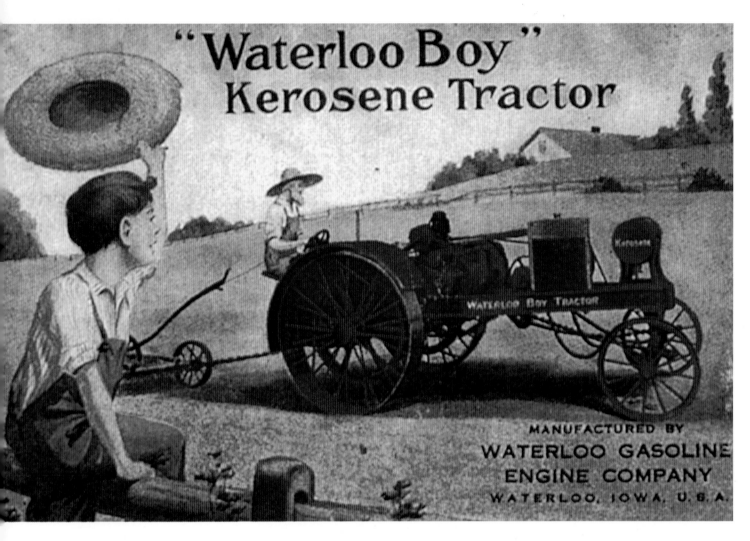

Waterloo Boy advertisement, 1914.

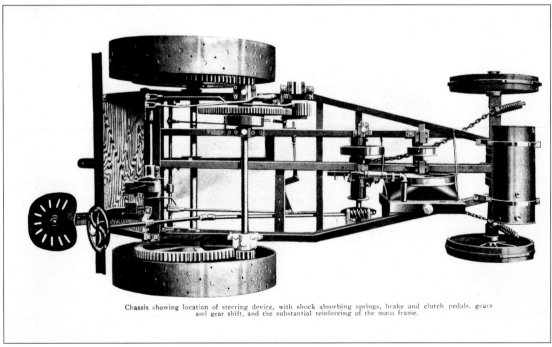

Chassis showing location of steering device, with shock absorbing springs, brake and clutch pedals, gears and gear shift, and the substantial reinforcing of the main frame.

Chassis of the Waterloo Boy.

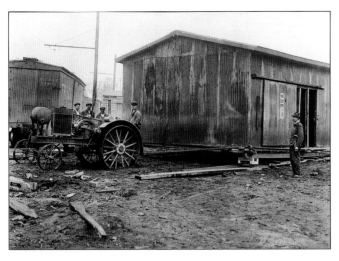

Deere workers use a Waterloo Boy to move buildings at the works in 1920.

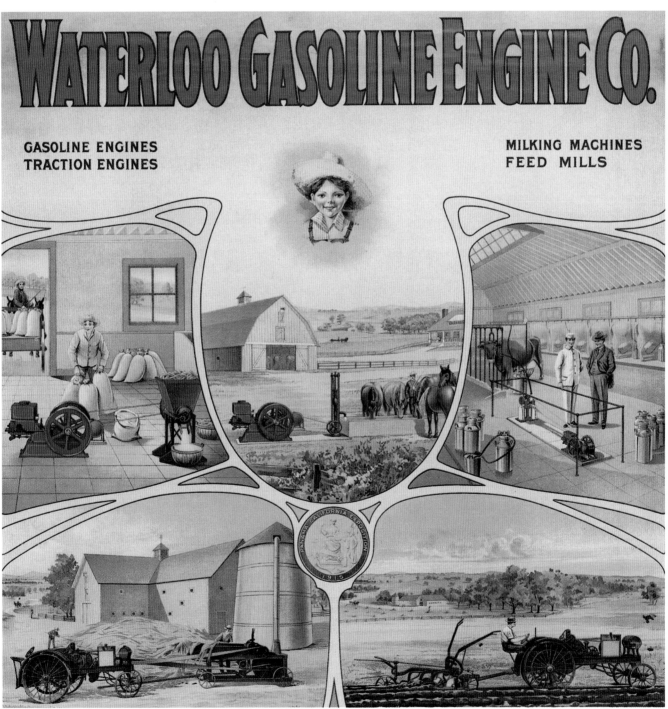

A 1915 Waterloo Gasoline Engine Company advertising poster.

Deere Experiments With Farm Tractors

Deere's board commissioned board member C. H. Melvin to build a tractor in 1912. Melvin's three-wheeler had two seats so it could be driven in either direction.

Deere's Experimental Department built these Motor Cultivators from 1916 to 1921.

S. H. Velie's Velie Motors of Moline produced its Biltwell tractors from 1916 to 1920. The firm was bought out by Deere on April 1, 1937.

Deere's Chief Engineer Max Sklovsky built this experimental tractor in 1916.

From the Dain to Deere's Waterloo Boy

In March 14, 1918, after Deere's own tractor design experiments during the previous four years resulted in the production of just 100 All-Wheel-Drive models designed by Joseph Dain, Deere purchased the Waterloo Gasoline Tractor Company, its tractors, patents, and works for $2,350,000. The Waterloo Boy was now Deere & Company's farm tractor.

Above: *A prototype of the Dain All-Wheel-Drive during field tests.*

Right: *Joseph Dain*

The Dain All-Wheel-Drive was produced in 1918 and 1919, but just 100 were built as the tractor cost some $1,700 instead of its goal price of $700.

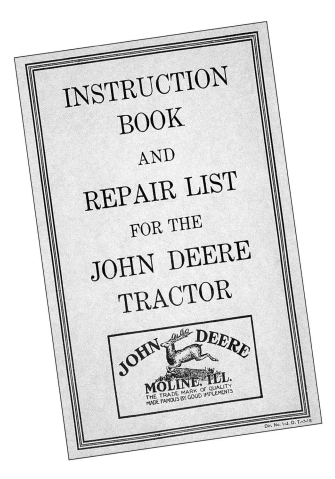

INSTRUCTION
BOOK
AND
REPAIR LIST
FOR THE
JOHN DEERE
TRACTOR

JOHN DEERE
MOLINE, ILL.
THE TRADE MARK OF QUALITY
MADE FAMOUS BY GOOD IMPLEMENTS

Dir. No. 1–J. D. T.–7-18

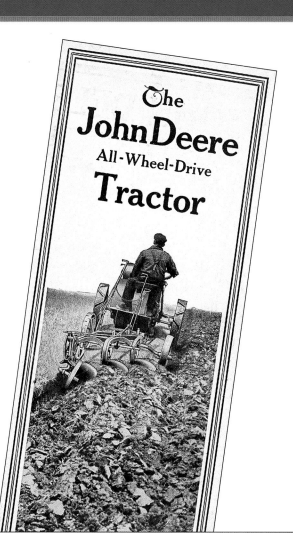

The
John Deere
All-Wheel-Drive
Tractor

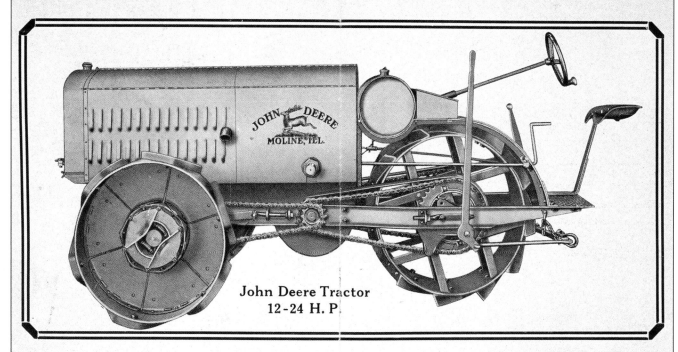

JOHN DEERE TRACTOR

John Deere Tractor
12-24 H. P.

The All-Wheel-Drive Tractor

John Deere's Tractor: The Waterloo Boy

A 1920 Waterloo Boy Model N fitted with a factory canopy inside the Waterloo works.

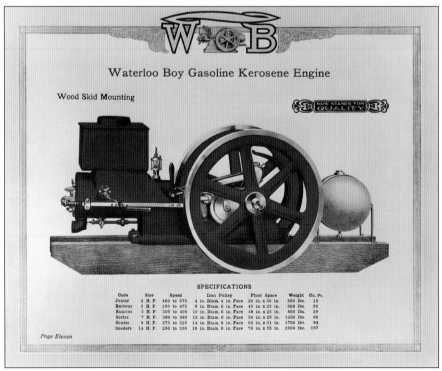

W·B

Waterloo Boy Gasoline Kerosene Engine

Wood Skid Mounting

NAME STANDS FOR QUALITY

SPECIFICATIONS

Code	Size	Speed	Iron Pulley	Floor Space	Weight	Cu. Ft.
Junior	2 H. P.	400 to 575	4 in. Diam. 4 in. Face	20 in. x 35 in.	350 lbs.	15
Ruivous	3 H. P.	550 to 475	6 in. Diam. 6 in. Face	40 in. x 23 in.	600 lbs.	30
Runices	5 H. P.	300 to 400	10 in. Diam. 6 in. Face	48 in. x 25 in.	850 lbs.	39
Sorios	7 H. P.	280 to 360	12 in. Diam. 6 in. Face	56 in. x 29 in.	1250 lbs.	66
Sonats	9 H. P.	275 to 325	14 in. Diam. 8 in. Face	62 in. x 31 in.	1700 lbs.	84
Sooders	14 H. P.	250 to 300	16 in. Diam. 8 in. Face	76 in. x 35 in.	2600 lbs.	107

Page Eleven

A restored Waterloo Boy Model N.

Working Overtime: England's Waterloo Boy

Some 4,000 of the two models were exported to Great Britain to help the World War I effort. The owner of the receiving company in London was L. J. Martin of the Overtime Tractor Company, and the machines were christened Overtime tractors.

THE NEW 30-H.P.

Overtime

NATIONAL FOOD PRODUCTION CAMPAIGN

CHAMPION TRACTOR OF ENGLAND AND WALES

WON BY THE OVERTIME TRACTOR

TWO-SPEED
FARM TRACTOR
1919 MODEL. "N."

"OVERTIME" FARM TRACTOR

Repairs & Instructions.

Stores Address:—
27 Goodman's Yard, Minories, E.C.

Offices:—
126-127 Minories, E.C.

May, 1917.

The **Overtime** FARM TRACTOR

PRICE £325

Above left: *A 1919 Overtime Model N brochure.*

Left: *A 1917 sales brochure and parts book for the Overtime Model R.*

Above: *An Overtime at work in England.*

Right: *A World War I–era advertisement for "The Champion Tractor of Great Britain."*

Inside the John Deere Works

Deere's plow works in 1924 had a dirt floor, gas lighting, and horse teams to haul around equipment.

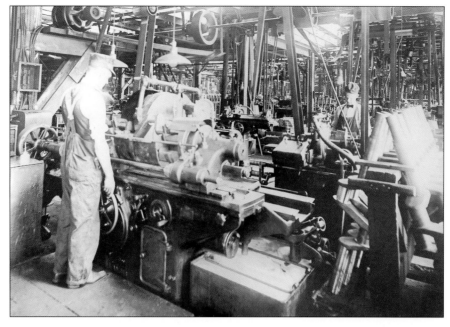

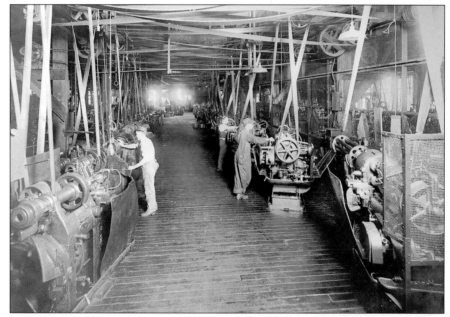

Above and left: *Lathes were run by drive belts from overhead drivelines.*

The foundry in Deere's Harvester Works.

The Farming Life in the 1910s

Sis and Junior stroke the muzzle of Ol'Dobbin, still the primary "horsepower" on many farms.

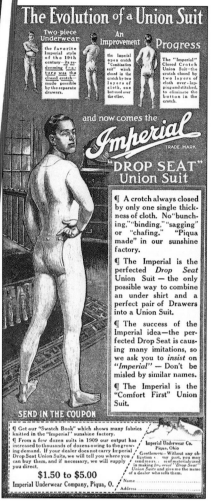

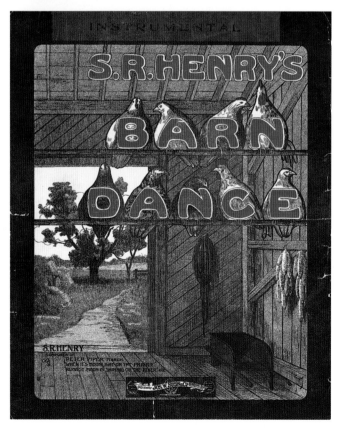

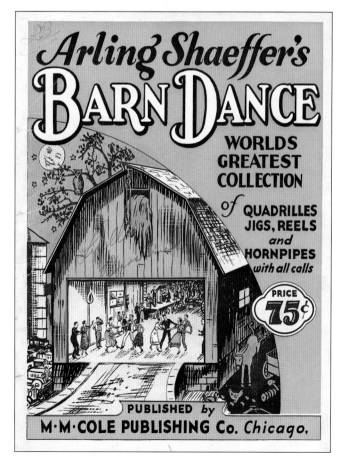

The Farming Life in the 1910s

Barn Raising
At Mr. J. Savey's
July 4, 1912
Frame — C. Geddes
Roland
Manitoba

Once upon a time, everyone in the area halted work on their own farms to come to the aid of a neighbor who needed a new barn raised. Workers accepted no pay beyond a hearty lunch befitting the labor they had put in and the assurance that others would reciprocate when the need arose.

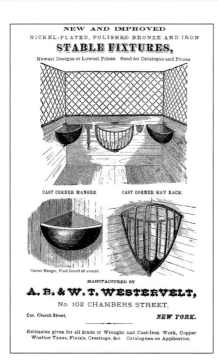

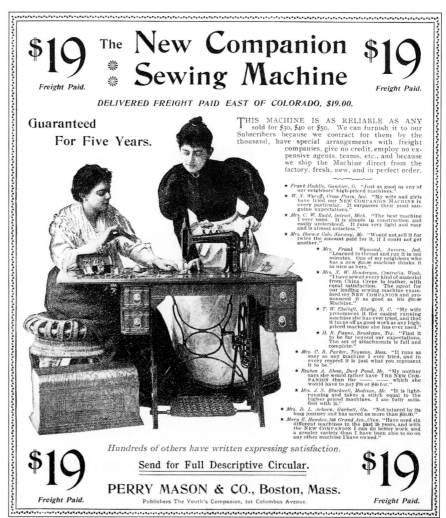

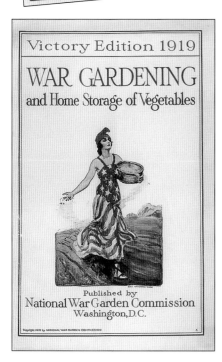

Above: *World War I–era Victory Garden cartoon.*

Left: *World War I brought on Victory Gardens with Lady Liberty sowing the seeds of freedom.*

Lanz and the Bulldog Tractor

Heinrich Lanz was born in Germany in 1838, just one year after John Deere crafted his first steel plow. Like Deere, Lanz saw a future in farming and began importing steam engines and threshing machines. In 1859, Lanz established his own factory in Mannheim and continued to add to his line of agricultural implements.

In 1902, Lanz visited the Deere works in Moline and met Charles Deere. This meeting sparked Lanz's enthusiasm for growth and paved the way for future cooperation between the two firms.

In 1921, Lanz's son, Karl, unveiled a stunning new tractor, the Bulldog, engineered by Dr. Fritz Huber as the world's first hot-bulb-fired tractor burning inexpensive crude oil. The Bulldog became a huge success for Lanz, with versions built throughout the world under license for decades thereafter.

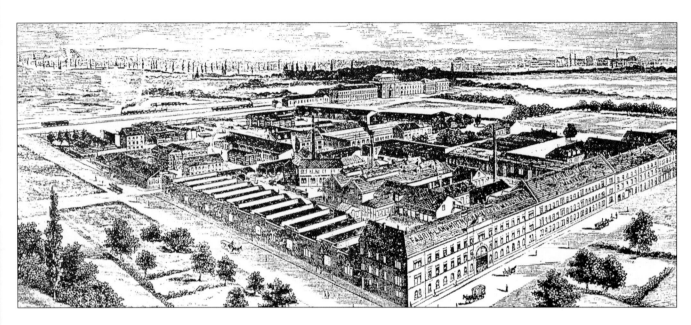

Above: *The Heinrich Lanz factory at Mannheim, Germany, 1870.*

Right: *A pioneering Lanz steam engine on a wheeled cart driving a Lanz thresher.*

Below: *A 1905 Lanz steam traction engine.*

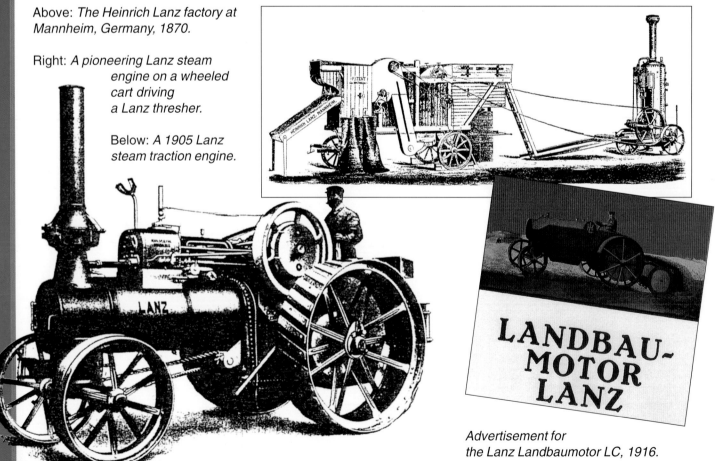

LANDBAU-MOTOR LANZ

Advertisement for the Lanz Landbaumotor LC, 1916.

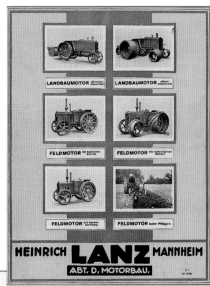

Above left: *Landbaumotor brochure, 1910s.*

Above: *The Landbaumotor Universal Motor Tiller, 1912.*

Far left: *An advertisement for Lanz's Landbaumotor, 1913.*

Left: *Lanz brochure showing its range of Landbaumotors and Feldmotors.*

Below: *Landbaumotor with attached Motor Tiller, 1915.*

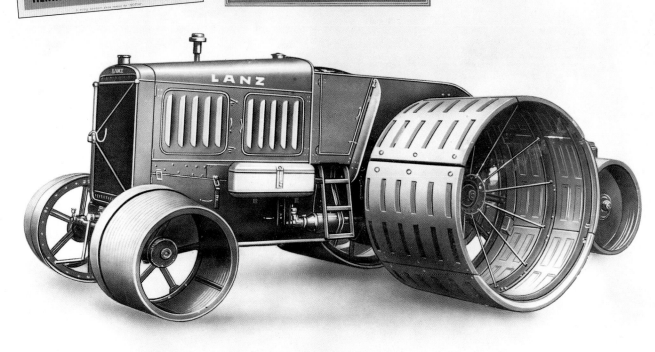

Lanz and the Bulldog Tractor

Early Lanz brochure for its Bulldog and Ackerbulldog models.

HEINRICH LANZ MANNHEIM
ABT. D. MOTORBAU.

BULLDOG, Stationär

BULLDOG mit Eisenbereifung

BULLDOG mit verbreiterten Hinterrädern

FILIALEN IN
BERLIN
BRESLAU
HAMBURG
HANNOVER
KÖLN a. Rh.
KÖNIGSBERG i.P.
LEIPZIG
REGENSBURG
WIEN
BUKAREST

VERTRETUNGEN
AN ALLEN
HAUPTPLÄTZEN
DES IN- UND
AUSLANDES
SOWIE
ÜBERSEE

BULLDOG mit Gummibereifung   ACKERBULLDOG

LANZ-FABRIKATE:
LOKOMOBILEN
für Satt- und Heissdampf,
fahrbar und stationär
DAMPFSTRASSENWALZEN
ZUGLOKOMOBILEN
BELEUCHTUNGS-
LOKOMOBILEN
DAMPFKESSEL

LANZ-FABRIKATE:
DRESCHMASCHINEN
für Hand-, Göpel-, Motor- und
Dampfbetrieb
SELBSTBINDER-PRESSEN
BALLENPRESSEN
FUTTER- UND RÜBEN-
SCHNEIDER
MAISREBLER
SCHROTMÜHLEN
GÖPEL

BULLDOG als Zugmaschine

D1

DER
NEUE 8 PS-
SCHWERÖLMOTOR
BULLDOG
(Telegramm-Bezeichnung: Mops)

Vielfachen Wünschen aus landwirtschaftlichen und gewerblichen Kreisen entsprechend, baue ich jetzt neben meinem 12-pferdigen Bulldog, der sich inzwischen in Landwirtschaft und Gewerbe glänzend eingeführt hat, auch einen 8 PS-Schwerölmotor „Bulldog"

DER 8 PS-BULLDOG
vereinigt in idealer Weise alle Ansprüche, die an eine moderne Kleinkraftmaschine gestellt werden.

Er ist:
Betriebssicher,   Stabil,   Leicht beweglich,
Einfach in der Bedienung,
Billig im Betrieb,
denn er begnügt sich mit minderwertigen, leicht zu beschaffenden Inland-Brennstoffen.

HEINRICH LANZ MANNHEIM

Bulldog 8-ps brochure.

Lanz Felddank powered by a two-cylinder benzene-fueled engine, 1923.

Far left: *Bulldog 12-ps brochure, 1921.*

Left: *Grossbulldog 22/28-ps brochure.*

Bulldog H Series tractor.

Building the Farm Machinery Line

Following the 1911 mergers, one final piece of the puzzle remained to be addressed: In 1912, the need for a binder was obvious if Deere & Company was to compete with its major rival, the International Harvester Company of Chicago, Illinois. In the winter of 1909–1910, the John Deere binder was designed by Harry J. Podlesak, an ex-employee of McCormick. Seven or eight machines were tried out in 1910; some 500 were built in 1911 in East Moline and a further 2,000 in 1912. During the summer of 1912, the first part of the new Deere Harvester Works was erected; it was completed in 1913. In 1914, some 12,000 binders were built.

During World War I, new Nos. 5 and 6 Pony plows with three to five bottoms were announced; they soon became the most popular plows for tractor use. These were joined by the Model 45 two-bottom plow with a special Model 40 for use with Henry Ford's ubiquitous and revolutionary Fordson tractor.

Both stiff-tooth and spring-tooth cultivators had been developed for both horses and tractors. Similarly, Pony disk harrows, both the famous Model B single-action and the double-action, rolling stalk cutters, and spike-tooth and plain harrows were all tillage equipment supplied for both. Syracuse produced their own spring-tooth float harrows.

On the haymaking front, the Dain factory, having moved several times, came to rest in Ottumwa, Iowa, to produce mowers, side-delivery and dump rakes, sweeps, stackers, and rake-bar loaders. Finally, hay presses were introduced, both standard models with 14x18- or 16x18-inch bales and a Junior press in the smaller size only. In addition to Dain's Iowa factory, another Dain works was built in 1909–1910 in Welland, Ontario, to cover the largest "local" export market, Canada, giving Deere a factory that still survives to date.

Another major member of the merger was Van Brunt. Builders of the most prestigious seed drills of the early twentieth century, it achieved a first in 1911 with a combined seed and fertilizer disk drill. Deere's drills carried the Van Brunt name through to World War II.

Deere's Van Brunt grain drill ready to work, 1919.

Left: *A duo of mule-drawn Deere riding cultivators work a cornfield, 1926.*

Below left: *Deere's Soil Culture Department was established in 1910 by Dr. Warren E. Taylor to offer helpful advice to farmers.*

Below: *Deere's Marseilles corn shellers expanded the harvesting line, 1912.*

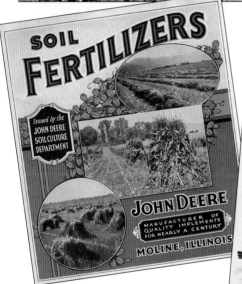

A Gas Traction Big Four 30 tractor pulls four Deere binders, 1912.

Entering a New Field: Deere and Automobiles

John Deere's grandson, Willard Velie, founded the Velie Carriage Company in Moline in 1901 building farm wagons and buggies. As times changed, he began in 1908 making horseless carriages with his first automobile, Old Maude.

Above: *Velie built more than 75,000 automobiles between 1908 and 1928, including this refined Coach Sedan of 1924.*

Right: *Deere-Clark's Type B automobile from 1907. The retail price was a mere $2,500.*

Above: *A Velie automobile down on the farm.*

Right: *For a brief interlude in 1906–1907, Charles Deere was president of Deere-Clark Motor Car Company. Deere-Clark sold several models of automobiles.*

TIMELINE

1912: Deere authorizes development of a gas-powered tractor plow as designed by C. H. Melvin. Work on Deere's tractor plow stops in 1914.

1912: The *Titanic* sinks. Oreo cookies are introduced.

1913: U.S. federal income tax is adopted. First crossword puzzle is created.

1914: World War I starts in Europe.

1915: Alfred Einstein publishes his *General Theory of Relativity*. The *Lusitania* is sunk by a German U-boat.

1916: Margaret Sanger starts the first U.S. birth-control clinic. The first U.S. self-service grocery store opens.

1917: Henry Ford's tractor, the Fordson, debuts, marking a milestone in tractor design, manufacture, and concept. Communist revolutionaries take over Russia.

1918: Deere buys the Waterloo Gas Engine Company, entering the tractor business. Daylight saving time is introduced. Canadian women are granted the right to vote.

1919: Deere's All-Wheel-Drive tractor, designed by Joe Dain, is built in East Moline. One hundred All-Wheel-Drive tractors are shipped and sold, but the design is abandoned as too expensive. Treaty of Versailles is signed ending World War I.

1920: Farmers make up 27 percent of the U.S. labor force with farms averaging 148 acres. U.S. Congress approves Prohibition, outlawing alcoholic beverages. U.S. women win the right to vote.

1921: Dr. Fritz Huber designs the semi-diesel hot-bulb Bulldog, Lanz's most famous tractor. The lie detector is invented.

1922: James Joyce publishes *Ulysses*. *Reader's Digest* magazine is created.

1923: Col. Jacob Schick patents the first electric shaver. *Time* magazine is founded.

CHAPTER 3

Johnny Popper Replaces the Horse, 1923–1937

Artist Walter Haskell Hinton's painting captured the farmwife's call to the table when she heard the sound of the "Poppin' Johnny."

Deere's Model D: The Trustworthy Poppin' Johnny

The era of unstyled tractors commenced for Deere & Company with the introduction of the famous Model D in 1923. The D was developed from the Waterloo Boy Models R and N. The Model D featured a good front-to-rear weight balance, and the established Waterloo Boy two-cylinder engine could lug down to its last breath. The new tractor proved itself without any doubt to be economical and easy for farmers to maintain themselves. As many old-timers attested, there was nothing quite like plowing with a Model D. The two-cylinder green machine was as hardy as a mule, as strong as an ox, and as trustworthy as a farm dog.

Right: *When Deere purchased the Waterloo Boy firm in 1918, Waterloo engineers were already at work on this Fordson-style tractor.*

Below: *Model D prototype, 1922. The Model D began life as a Waterloo Boy, following the Deere engineers' updates of the Model N Styles A, B, and C.*

JOHN DEERE FARM TRACTOR
MODEL D 15-27

THE SIMPLE TRACTOR THAT IS LIGHT IN WEIGHT AND SMALL IN
DIMENSIONS, BUT BIG IN POWER

Model D 15/27, 1925.

Above: *A Deere field demonstrator shows off his Model D near Lincoln, Nebraska, in 1926.*

Right: *Model D brochure, 1927.*

Engineering the Model D

The man behind Joseph Dain's All-Wheel-Drive tractor was a graduate engineer from Champaign, Illinois, named Elmer McCormick. After Dain died suddenly of pneumonia and production of the All-Wheel-Drive was halted, Deere purchased rights to the Waterloo Boy, and McCormick became a Deere salesman. But his engineering background prompted him to work on the Waterloo Boy, and soon he developed what became the Model D tractor.

The sound of Deere's two-cylinder engines was so distinctive, farm wives could tell from the note of the engine when their husbands had idled down the tractor to come in for supper.

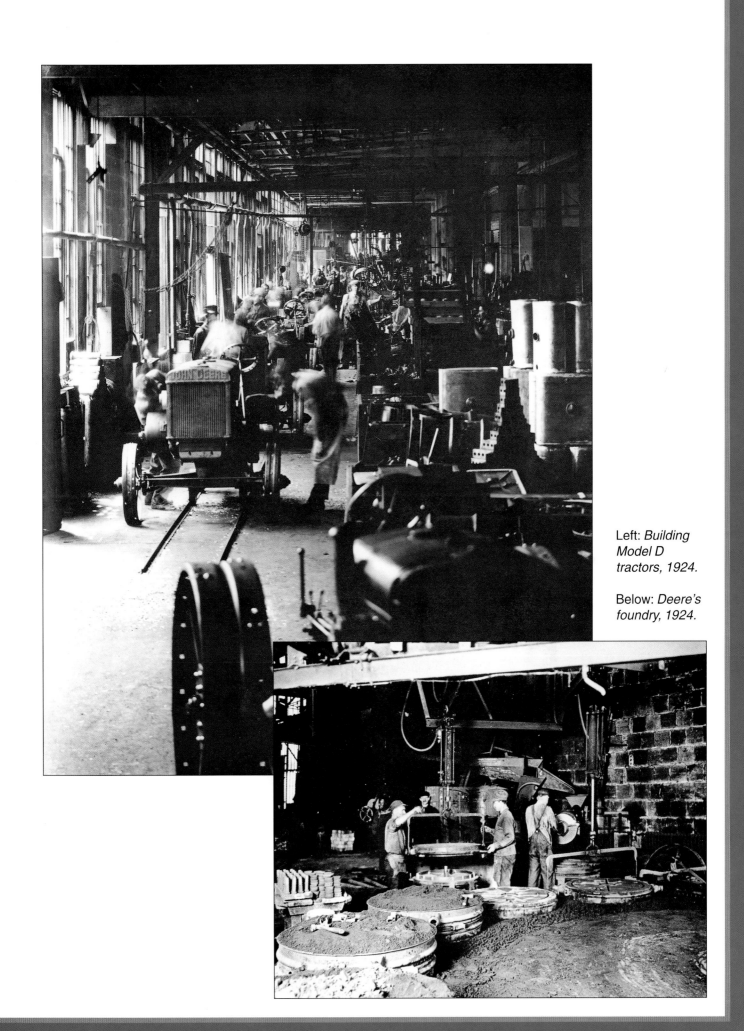

Left: *Building Model D tractors, 1924.*

Below: *Deere's foundry, 1924.*

Farming With the Model D

Left: *A farmer shovels his Model D out of a mudpit—an all-too-common mishap in wet fields.*

Below: *And when day was done, the Model D was a fine resting spot to look back on work accomplished.*

Contract for the purchase of Deere equipment, 1924.

Naturally Junior wanted a Johnny Popper of his own!

The Farming Life in the 1920s

Ma and Pa proudly display their blue-ribbon bull.

Battery-powered radios came to the farm, bringing entertainment, ag prices, and immediate news of the world to farm families.

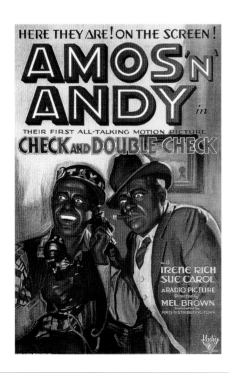

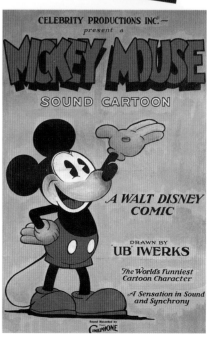

From the Model C to the Model GP

With the debut of International Harvester's Farmall in 1924, Deere rushed to expand its tractor line. The success of the Model D inevitably meant that a demand was created for a smaller model. Engineer Elmer McCormick continued his work, developing Deere's first row-crop tractor, the Model C of 1927. It was soon updated as the GP.

A tricycle version of the Model GP was also engineered, first as a Tricycle GP and then as the GPWT Series, with a special version for potatoes, the Model P. Another development for orchard work was the GPO, and from it the Lindeman brothers in Yakima, Washington, built a few crawler versions known to collectors as the GPO-Lindeman.

Top: *Deere Model C, 1928. Development of the general-purpose Model C began in 1926.*

Above: *A Model C pulls a Deere corn picker, tended by a team of mules pulling a wagon, 1928.*

JOHN DEERE GENERAL-PURPOSE FARM TRACTOR

The GENERAL-PURPOSE TRACTOR OF STANDARD DESIGN THAT DOES ALL FARM WORK WITHIN ITS POWER RANGE

Left: *Model C brochure, 1929.*

Right: *Even Fido was enamored with the Poppin' Johnny.*

A Model GP powers a grinder, 1928. The Model C became the GP after Deere worried that the model names "D" and "C" would be confused on the telephone.

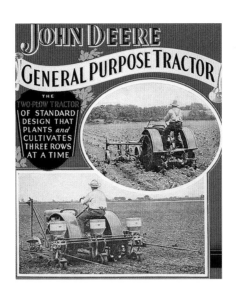

Model GP brochure, 1930.

Model GPWT brochure, 1931.

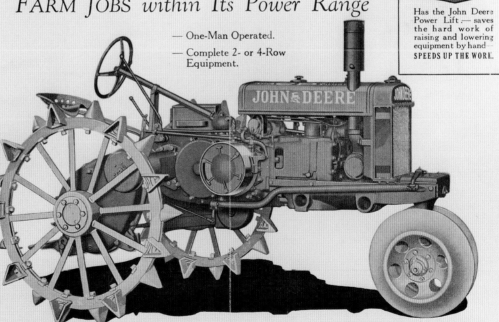

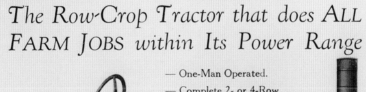

Above: *The tricycle Model GPWT, 1930.*

Left: *A Model GPWT fitted with a Deere Model 400 corn and cotton planter, 1929.*

1929 Model GP with mounted 7-foot sickle bar Tractor Mower

This 1929 Model GP and integral Tractor Mower could make hay quickly while the sun shone. The GP's built in power-takeoff shaft drove the mower's 7-foot sickle bar back and forth through its pointed guards to cut hay, weeds, stubble, or pasture. When the mower was lowered into cutting position, the sharpened A-shaped sickle sections mounted on the reciprocating bar cut the crop. A Power Lift exclusive to the GP Models helped raise and lower the bar. Designed as Deere's first all-crop or general-purpose tractor, it was introduced in 1928. The GP was produced until 1935, when the Models A and B tricycle-type tractor designs took its place. Owners: Phyllis and Wayne Pokorny. (Photograph © Ralph W. Sanders)

The Tractor Heard Around the World:

Developing Deere's General Purpose Tractor

By Wayne G. Broehl Jr.

There had been one significant shortcoming of all the gasoline tractors built before 1924—a lack of versatility. They could not be used for many farm tasks that agriculturalists might wish to convert to tractor power. Farmers had been using their tractors to prepare seedbeds (plowing, disking, harrowing) and probably for some harvesting (especially the cutting of small grains). Tractors were also enormously helpful in driving other pieces of machinery—in threshing, silo filling, feed grinding, wood sawing, baling, shelling, shredding. But these tasks were only part of a farmer's spectrum of horsepower needs, for with all of the row crops—corn, hay, cotton, kafir, potatoes, tobacco, peas, peanuts, beans, sugar beets—not only the cultivation but generally the planting was done by horse. In the way tractors were constructed, it was not very easy to drive them down a row to plant or cultivate. Similarly, many functions in the harvest were more readily accomplished by horse—mowing hay, cutting corn, digging potatoes, etc. One industry executive in 1924 maintained that the tractors in use replaced on an average only 2.8 horses per tractor (though he did admit that owners of larger tractors often disposed of six to eight horses upon purchase of the tractor). A U.S. Department of Agriculture bulletin of 1925 graphically showed the relatively small part of the total horsepower need assumed by the gasoline tractor in that period—only 1.6 billion of 16 billion horsepower hours, work animals providing 9.7 billion horsepower hours.

The incredible potential for the tractor cultivation of row crops was just waiting for an innovative idea. Indeed, it seemed anomalous that after more than two decades of gasoline-tractor development, no one had been able to perfect such a row-crop tractor. But 1924 brought a solution, a very successful new four-cylinder tractor from the industry leader, International Harvester. Its name ideally described the essence of the need—the Farmall.

In construction, the Farmall differed radically from other tractors. Its rear axle was built high, with a clearance of thirty inches above the ground, and the larger rear drive wheels were wide apart (seventy-four inches between the centers of the wheels); it could clear corn or cotton as well as the ordinary riding cultivator, and the wheels were wide enough apart to straddle two rows and thus cultivate two rows at a time. The front wheels, some twenty-five inches in diameter, were located close together in order to run between the two rows. A particularly attractive feature to the farmer was the placement of the International Harvester cultivator, out in front of the tractor where the operator could watch the work. The Farmall also filled a real need in planting, being able to plant either two or four rows at a time.

It is difficult to overemphasize the breakthrough in farming technology brought by this one new tractor. The response from the field was instantaneous—the Farmall became an abiding success. It was patently clear to the farmer that the Farmall could do things that the Fordson could not do, that the Deere Model D could not do.

The remarkable dominance of the Fordson tractor in the early 1920s—70 percent of all gasoline tractors in 1922, 76 percent in 1923, 71 percent in 1924—now began to decline. Though Henry Ford still commanded more than 50 percent of all gasoline tractors produced in 1926, the onrush of the International Harvester Farmall that year soon reversed the figures. By 1928 there were only 12,500 Fordsons produced, and late in that year Henry Ford gave up making Fordsons in the United States (although he

Grandpa tells Junior how times have changed with the arrival of Deere's Model D.

did continue to make them in Cork, Ireland, and Dagenham, England). The Fordson was not adaptable to row-crop farming and that must have been one factor, among many, that persuaded Ford to retire from domestic competition in tractors, a surprising decision in retrospect, given his preeminence just a few years earlier. By 1928 International Harvester had moved into a commanding position, building more than 47 percent of all farm tractors that year and almost 60 percent in 1929.

The row-crop tractors did not replace their larger counterparts, of course, and International Harvester continued to make its famous Titan 10-20 tractor and its larger version, the 15-30. Nevertheless, the advent of the Farmall gave International Harvester a competitive edge that brought its dominance in the tractor field to an all-time high. It was an epochal step for the industry.

Deere & Company had entered the tractor field quite late and did so over the grudging opposition of many of its management—William Butterworth, George Crampton, and others. The precipitous decline of the Waterloo Boy right after World War I had been offset by the development at Waterloo of the first commercially viable Deere tractor, the Model D. This machine was an instant market success. Leon Clausen had almost single-handedly ensured that the Model D would be made in enough quantity to give it a good field test; at this point he left the company, thus placing the tractor's future in the hands of Charles Wiman.

Wiman had no doubts about the Model D's viability, and in 1925 he pushed production to more than 3,900 tractors. Further, he quickly committed the company to an all-crop tractor. Theo Brown was given the responsibility in 1925 for designing the machine with the help of a number of Waterloo engineers, particularly H. E. McCray and J. E. Cade, aided by H. B. McKahin, the Planter Works manager.

Right at the start, Brown made an important design decision that was to prove highly controversial—to enable Deere's all-crop tractor to handle a three-row cultivator. McKahin, meanwhile, had gone to Texas to test an International Harvester Farmall that Deere had purchased. He reported back that it could handle both two-row cultivators and four-row versions, and he commented somberly, "A three-row is not going to be popular there as the rows have to be watched to make sure that the old stalks do not drag."

By July 1926, three prototype tractors had been built that could pull a two-bottom plow (both the earlier Waterloo Boy and the Model D were designed for three-bottom plows). There was one especially striking innovation on the tractor—Brown and his colleagues had developed a power lift mechanism that would raise the integral tools of the cultivator or planter by engine power rather than mechanically by operator levers. Thus it had four forms of power—drawbar, belt, power take-off, and power lift. The latter became an "industry first," soon widely adopted in similar forms by competitors.

Within a few weeks the new Deere cultivator arrived to be tested on the all-crop tractor. Brown felt encouraged: "In the afternoon we had the outfit in the field and there is no question but what the outfit followed the ground in fine shape. The swinging frame is fine and is necessary. The lost motion has been taken out of the steering gear, which helps. We had Farmall out too, and in crossing corn we have the advantage of quicker dodge and rather better view ahead. On straight-way Farmall may be a little better, but McCray thinks we are nearly equal and in respect to crossing corn, better. . . . It really seems as though the idea of our cultivator is right and that we are on the right track. It is really encouraging."

By this time the Farmall was in the International Harvester dealers' shops and there was mounting pressure from Deere branches to "get the new tractor into our hands." Wiman feared a misfire by premature release of the prototypes (a la George Peek's Universal tractor fiasco), and he cautioned the board: "Development work of this kind is rather a slow process. . . . This was the best way to proceed, rather than to place the machine on the market before proper field and experimental work had been taken care of."

So further tinkering was done on a number of features of the tractor and it was once more tested early in the crop season of 1927. The test site was Mercedes, Texas, and again the Farmall and the All-Crop competed side by side. Brown reported the tester's reaction: "Hornberg said that he never thought corn could be cultivated with a tractor, but now he thinks it can be, and much faster. However, he is not yet convinced that the three-row idea is right."

The prototypes were also tested by a Decatur, Illinois, farm family, C. C. Veech and his sons. The former put the problem of the three-row cultivator bluntly: "Never believed in a two-row cultivator as a man had all he could do to run and watch a single row . . . could see the tractor and planter but not the cultivator . . . the boys could try it, but did not expect to let them cultivate a whole row but would have to tell them to take it out . . . had horses ready to go and do the job. However, the boys cultivated one row and then another, and then told the boys to go ahead and cultivate with a three-row . . . frankly surprised to find out how well the three-row did . . . would say, as did sons, that the cultivator seemed to be okay."

Wiman agonized over what was obviously a calculated risk—that the concept of three-row cultivation would not be effective. The alternative—to scrap the prototypes and begin afresh—was unpalatable. Wiman

Above: *Deere's tractor line on show at the Indian State Fair, 1920s.*

Left: *Taking up where John Froelich left off, a Model D powers a full threshing crew, 1930.*

Right: *The Model D's enclosed gears were one of the tractor's advances, adopted in 1923.*

Below: *A Model D pulls a Deere binder, 1930.*

warned the board of the opportunity costs of this: "Redesign of the Model 'C' to a so-called little Model 'D' tractor would keep us two years away in point of time from production on such a cheaper two-plow tractor. . . . It seems that our best opportunity, considering everything such as time, economy of manufacture of one model only, supplying to our dealers a reasonably full line of tractors, would dictate that our best procedure now was to manufacture the Model 'C' as a two-plow tractor and should the all-crop feature fail, then proceed to lay out a little Model 'D'."

If the new model was to be built, space would be needed either at Waterloo or elsewhere. If only existing space was used at Waterloo, the 100-tractor-a-day schedule for the Model D would have to be cut back—and just at the point when demand for the D was going up. If the Model D schedules were to be maintained, probably even expanded, then separate additional factory space would be needed for the new model. Wiman estimated the cost of additional space and of its tooling to be more than $3 million, but he pointed out that "even though we should go so far as to abandon the All-Crop idea and go to a small D machine, all of the machinery and tools would be useful, except possibly 10 percent of the original appropriation. . . ." It was the time loss in such an abandonment that would be costly.

After extensive testing over the spring and summer of 1927, considerable questions still remained about whether the three-row cultivator was the right configuration. C. C. Webber wrote from Minnesota: "It worked better than he expected it would work, and you assure us that the men who are running the tractor find it easier than driving a two-row cultivator." Webber then added an upsetting observation: "You have not the power at the present time to pull this three-row cultivator under all of conditions-that we presume you realize."

The question of the tractor's power had made everyone uneasy right from the start, and doubly so when McCray reported in late 1927 about a test on hilly ground. "Straight up on side hills Model C was okay, but sideways not as good as IHC 10-20." Theo Brown confided to his diary: "At meeting in afternoon it was decided to go ahead with Model C, having in mind that it was not equal in power on hills to IHC 10-20. Also, it was decided to design on paper a two-bottom tractor, simply as a plowing job that could be sold for $775 to the farmer. Silloway and Lourie are strong for the General Purpose tractor. Minneapolis wants a two-bottom plowing tractor only."

Frank Silloway, speaking from the sales manager's perspective, argued persuasively for building the full complement of the Ds and Cs, and doing it in Waterloo. Others on the board, notably the often conservative George Crampton, argued against it: "I am very much averse to putting any more money in Waterloo for brick and mortar."

C. C. Webber had the final word: "The tractor business is so definitely connected with the other tools in our line that I think we must protect the interests of stockholders and be prepared to supply the demand. We have suffered very much by not having sufficient tractors this year. We must meet the situation and I would favor the program." Wiman, still harboring many personal misgivings about the new tractor, moved that $3.9 million be expended for new buildings at Waterloo and the board passed the measure without further argument. The die had been cast.

Silloway now decided to rename the tractor and at first considered a popularized name—two suggestions were "Powerfarmer" and "Farmrite." He worried about detracting from the Model D, however: "If we were to name either tractor 'Powerfarmer,' we would give that name to our real power farmer tractor, the Model D. . . . We do not care to popularize with a name such as 'Powerfarmer,' the smaller tractor on which we make little profit, as against the Model D which is a profitable tractor for both the dealer and ourselves to sell and the one that most farmers should buy."

Silloway finally decided against a trade name and told the branches why: "Some of the branch houses have objected to Model 'C'. . . . 'D' and 'C' both have the sound of ee. When the dealer orders a tractor over the telephone, it would be very easy for a misunderstanding to arise because of the similarity in sound." Silloway chose the initials "GP," to stand for "general purpose." In the process, the term "all-crop" was discarded.

By October 1928 the production of the GP tractors was up to about twenty-five per day. But at this point Wiman reported to the board about an unsettling development: "For some unknown reason the horsepower had not been up to expectations. It was hoped that the tractor would develop at least 25-horsepower in order to give proper feel of performance but the dynamometer test has indicated that some of the tractors have developed only from 20 to 22 horsepower. The last 300 tractors show on dynamometer tests, 22.6 HP (belt)." Brown was with Wiman in that week and reported: "He is very blue because there has been complaint that the GP tractor is short of power. It seems to me this should be rectified as soon as possible. He is discouraged (too easily) and thinks we should build a regular two-plow tractor. All this is disturbing." Wiman even brought the issue to the board, telling them that he had "given some thought to the proposition of making a straight two-plow tractor to be known as the Model B to either replace the GP or be an addition to the line. Such a tractor would have many parts in common with the D but would only pull a two-bottom plow."

Wiman had been the hell-for-leather advocate for the combine, and at that time Webber had demurred. Now the roles seemed reversed. Webber urged the board: "Regardless of the consideration being given to the Model B or two-plow tractor, no efforts should be spared towards completing the job with a GP tractor as this . . . [is] absolutely necessary before going to the two-plow machine." Wiman finally deferred to Webber's judgment.

As if this was not enough, horsepower concerns relating to the Model D now surfaced. The D's horsepower had been improved a bit in 1928 with the addition of a ¼-inch increase in the cylinder bore and an improved carburetor, resulting in an increase in the drawbar horsepower to about twenty-eight, and thirty-six horsepower on the belt. Unfortunately, Wiman reported, "No more horsepower could be built into our present Model D tractor without a pretty thorough redesign throughout . . . this tractor is now up to its limit of strength and stability with the horsepower delivered to the drawbar as at present. . . . If the I.H.C. is able to beat us in the field on field performance . . . we will have to rely on our selling of these machines in volume on the greater simplicity of the Model D tractors, its two-cylinder construction and its reputation as a low-cost machine from an economy standpoint and from the non-use of a large number of repairs."

The horsepower fears were exacerbated when in January 1929 Deere learned that International Harvester had also incorporated a ¼-inch increase in the bore of the cylinder of their 15-30 tractor, which it was rumored would add anywhere from five to twelve horsepower to the machine. This worried Deere not only because of the disappointing horsepower of the GP, but also as a direct assault on the Model D. Inasmuch as the D was the large-production star of the Deere line, any threat to its sales was even more serious. Wiman reported to the board: "It is unfortunate that this vicious circle or race for horsepower has again been started, but it is not strange when you consider the fact that for the last two years we have been able to outperform the International 15-30 machine, that they should increase the speed and power on their machines to equal or better our own. To sell their old 15-30's on the territory, the International Company have cut the price of this machine $100 and we believe this will have to be cut further yet."

With the renewed threat from the 15-30's increased horsepower, Silloway decided to reemphasize the competitive advantages of the Model D and issued a bulletin headed, "John Deere, a two-cylinder tractor." The memorandum bluntly denied that Deere was thinking of shifting to a four-cylinder tractor. "Why should we?" Silloway wrote, "The John Deere two-cylinder tractors will do plowing and other field work at the lowest possible cost per acre and, after all, that is what the farmer is interested in." Silloway emphasized the light weight that led to fuel economy, the extreme simplicity, with its low cost of upkeep, and the fact that the owner could do his own servicing.

Detractors of the two-cylinder concept often used as their argument the excessive vibration of a two-cylinder motor. But Deere counteracted this attack by sending a Model D tractor to fairs, mounting the machine on four pop bottles, and putting the tractor in operation with the rear wheels turning. There was not enough rhythmic vibration to shake the machine off the mouths of the bottles.

Wiman's skepticism about the GP was soon confirmed by reactions from farmers. To start with, there were a number of breakdowns in operation, requiring rebuilding of some of the tractors in the field. Even more important was the farmer reaction to the three-row cultivating feature. While many farmers in the cornbelt seemed to accept the notion reasonably well, the cotton growers in the South clearly preferred two- and four-row operations. There were also inherent design problems; one was visibility for the driver on the GP. "It seems to me that the view is the real problem now. The Farmall has the best of us there," noted Theo Brown. Wayne H. Worthington, in his definitive study of the agricultural tractor for the Society of Automotive Engineers, succinctly summed up the reputation of the GP: "Unfortunately, the three-row idea failed in its acceptance and the tractor fell far short of Model D performance and durability."

Within a year, Brown and his development team were back at the drawing boards trying to rectify the GP's problems. A crash program soon brought into production a variation of the GP—the GP Wide-Tread. In many respects it was similar to its predecessor except that it had a long rear axle that allowed the machine to straddle two rows and the first John Deere tricycle front to run between two rows, just as the Farmall did. By the crop season of 1929, the GP Wide-Tread was available to buy and its acceptance not only in the South but in the Midwest was more gratifying. In 1931 the GP itself was modified to raise its horsepower ratings to 15.52 drawbar, 24.30 belt-pulley. A year later, in 1932, the GP Wide-Tread was modified to provide a tapered hood to increase the visibility of the driver and to provide changes in the steering apparatus that prevented the tendency of the front wheels to whip on rough ground. With the second model of the GP, and the modifications and additional features, the GP finally made a respectable showing in the Deere line. Charles Wiman always remembered his experience with the GP, however, as "an outstanding failure" and often mentioned: "Well do I recall how much tractor business was lost by our company due to bad design of the 'GP' line."

A restored Deere Model D. (Photographs by Hans Halberstadt)

TIMELINE

1923: Deere announces its all-new Model D, the first of the long line of "Johnny Poppers."

1924: Farmall tractor is introduced by International Harvester, spurring other tractor makers to build row-crop machines. Soybeans grow as a prominent crop.

1925: Scotch tape is invented.

1926: Ford introduces the forty-hour work week to curb overproduction and limit unemployment.

1926: Hybrid seed corn becomes available, dramatically boosting yields.

1927: Deere launches its combine line with the Model No. 2. Charles Lindbergh flies *The Spirit of St. Louis* from New York to Paris. Philo T. Farnsworth invents television. Kool-Aid is introduced. The first "talking" movie, *The Jazz Singer*, debuts.

1928: Alexander Fleming discovers penicillin.

1928: Deere GP is introduced as a three-row "all-crop" tractor. Charles Deere Wiman, great-grandson of John Deere, is named company president. Otto Rohwedder invents sliced bread. Walt Disney introduces Mickey Mouse. Gerber's baby food debuts. Bubble gum is invented.

1929: The stock market crash sparks the Great Depression.

The Mechanical Mule: Debut of the Model A

During 1932, experiments were in process to develop the last series GPWT with its over-hood steering into a more advanced, row-crop model. In 1932, the experimental FX, followed by the GX later in the year, led the way for the development.

In 1933, some eight models were built, designated as the AA: two known as the AA-3 featured three-speed gear-boxes and six termed the AA-1 had four-speed transmissions. The three-speed was soon discarded, but the next four pre-production tractors were successful enough to justify the announcement of the new Model A for 1934. The first 4,800 had an open fanshaft.

In 1935, a single-front-wheel AN version was introduced, followed by an AW with wide-adjustable-front axle.

Right: *Model AA prototype with mounted cultivator, 1933.*

Below: *An early Model A with an open fanshaft, 1934.*

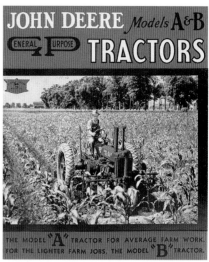

A Model A works a cornfield with an A492 mounted cultivator, 1937.

Models A and B brochure, 1936.

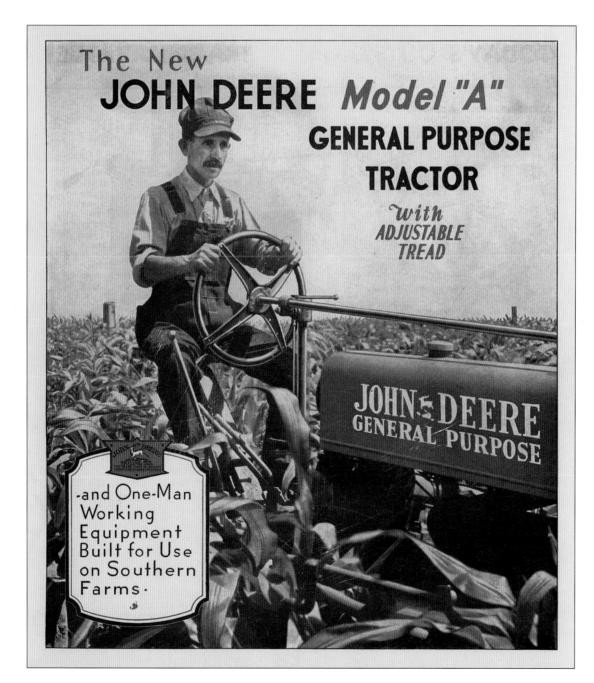

Model A brochure.

1937 John Deere Model A with mounted two-row cultivator

Cultivating two crop rows was a breeze for this 1937 John Deere Model A tractor and its mounted hydraulic-lift cultivator. And an umbrella over the driver gave some relief from long hours in the sun. First introduced in 1934, the Model A offered many improvements over earlier Deere tractors. The wheel tread could be adjusted to different row widths by sliding the wheel hubs on a long splined axle. Some models were equipped with a hydraulic power lift that helped raise implements. Burning kerosene or distillate fuel, the original A had 18.72 drawbar and 24.71 belt hp— enough for two 16-inch plow bottoms. On rubber tires, the early As could handle three 14-inch plow bottoms in most soils. Owners: Phyllis and Wayne Pokorny. (Photograph © Ralph W. Sanders)

101

The Mechanical Mule: Debut of the Model A

Right: *A later Model AO cultivates an orchard.*

Below: *A restored Model AO. (Photograph by Hans Halberstadt)*

An Ertl 1/16-scale Precision Series Model A.

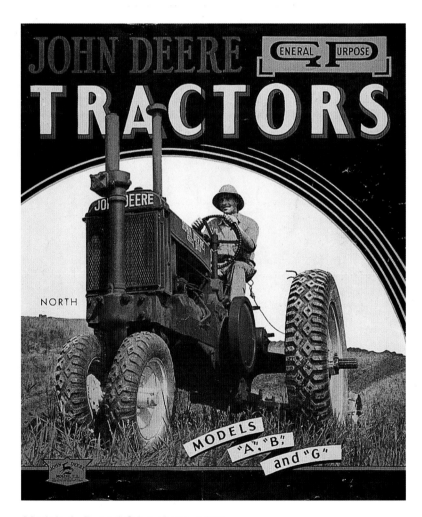

Models A, B, and G brochure, 1938.

Timeline

1930: Farmers make up 21 percent of the U.S. labor force with farms averaging 157 acres. One farmer now supplies food for 9.8 persons in the U.S. and abroad. 15–20 labor-hours are required to produce 100 bushels of corn with two-bottom gang plow, 7-foot tandem disk, four-section harrow, and two-row planters, cultivators, and pickers. 58 percent of U.S. farms now have cars, 34 percent have telephones, and 13 percent have electricity. Hostess introduces the Twinkie.

1931: Caterpillar builds the first diesel farm tractor. The world's tallest building, the Empire State Building, opens in New York City.

1932: Franklin Delano Roosevelt becomes U.S. president. Air conditioning is invented. Pneumatic rubber tires are factory supplied on tractors by Allis-Chalmers. Deere soon follows the trend.

1933: Prohibition is repealed. Loch Ness monster is first spotted.

1934: Deere launches its best-selling tractors of all time, the Models A and B. Adolf Hitler takes power in Germany. Parker Brothers debuts Monopoly.

1935: Social Security Act is passed by U.S. Congress.

1936: Deere acquires Caterpillar's combine line. Electrical power is available on most U.S. farms under the Rural Electrification Administration. Farm families are soon using running water, refrigerators, freezers, electric stoves, toasters, water heaters, vacuum cleaners, irons, and clothes washers as well as milking machines, electric motors to grind and deliver feed, and to pump water for animals.

1937: Deere celebrates its centennial. Despite the Great Depression, the company achieved $100 million in gross sales for the first time. Deere introduces two new tractors on opposite ends of the power spectrum, the Models G and 62, which became the L. Amelia Earhart is lost over the Pacific. The *Hindenburg* crashes. Spam is introduced.

1937 Model AW
with No. 290 planter

The adjustable front axle for wide spacing of the front wheels earned the AW its distinction as a model separate from the Model A. The AW operates like the A and can pull two or three plows. The round-spoke French & Hecht wheels came with factory-equipped rubber tires. Fenders were optional. This AW pulls a Deere No. 290 two-row high-speed check-row planter. When dropping corn in check-rowed hills, the planter could seed at 5 mph. A button-studded wire that stretched across the field released the seed from the planter. Passing through the planter mechanism, each button dropped a hill of corn at an interval equal to the row width. Corn planted in this way could be cultivated with the row and across the row, providing good weed control. Owner: Jim Finnigan. (Photograph © Ralph W. Sanders)

The Little Sibling: Arrival of the Model B

Late in 1934, the smaller Model B joined the line with similar optional front ends to the Model A. The first 41,134 Model B tractors had a short front-support frame. This was extended at serial number 42200 to allow mid-mounted equipment to be interchangeable with the A models. It was 1937 before Hi-Crop versions of both the Models A and B were introduced as the ANH, AWH, BNH, and BWH, as well as a special narrow model, the BWH-40 of which only six were built.

Also in 1935, three standard-tread types of both models were introduced: the AR and BR for wheatland use, the low-stance AO and BO for orchard and grove, and the AI and BI, suitably reinforced for industrial work. The standard unstyled D was similarly available in DO and DI formats. For five years from 1936 to 1940, the orchard A was streamlined to become the AOS, but reverted to the AO when it received a larger engine in 1941.

A narrow-front Model BN.

Above: *A Model B fitted pneumatic rubber tires cuts hay.*

Top right: *Models A and B brochure.*

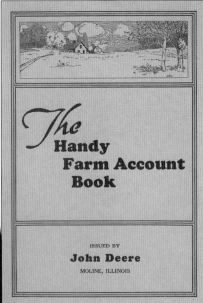

A Model B powers a Deere No.10 corn picker over a never-ending field, 1935. With the advent of pneumatic rubber tires for tractors, Deere was quick to offer them on its machines.

A Love Affair with Johnny Poppper

By the mid-1920s, Deere's green farm tractors were inexpensive enough that most every farmer could afford one and refined enough that it didn't take a wizard with a wrench to operate it. "Power farming" was here to stay. And along the way, the special sound of the two-cylinder Deere also worked its way into farmers' hearts. It was a simple mechanical noise that you could trust and believe in, and Deeres became lovingly known as Poppin' Johnnies and Johnny Poppers, the tractor that replaced the horse.

Model BO, 1935.

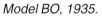

A restored Model BO. (Photograph by Hans Halberstadt)

A Model BR at work, 1935.

Lindeman-John Deere Crawler Tractor with hydraulic tool bar-mounted in front position. Equipped with Lindeman 6-foot dozer blade and depth adjustment shoe. Blade shown in raised position.

LINDEMAN POWER EQUIPMENT CO.
YAKIMA, WASH.

Above: *The Lindeman Power Equipment Company converted Model BO wheeled tractors to crawlers. This one is fitted with a hydraulic blade.*

Right: *Model BO-L leaflet.*

A Model BO-L at work in a hilly orchard.

Launching the Models A and B Tractors

By Wayne G. Broehl Jr.

Charles Wiman had no doubts about basic product research. Of all Wiman's management decisions during the Great Depression, the one that was probably most long lasting in effect was his decision to aggressively continue new product development through the worst days of the downturn. Already the Model D tractor was highly popular with the trade—the company had sold more than 100,000 units by 1930 and would keep the model in the product line twenty-three more years after this date. The GP and its companion, GP-Wide Tread, had not done as well, though more than 35,000 would eventually be made before the latter was terminated in 1933, the former in 1935. Still, competition from the other companies constrained one from resting on laurels with one good model and two somewhat limping models. Also, it was becoming increasingly apparent that farmers around the country were avidly looking for many improvements—adjustable tread widths in the rear wheels, less side draft in the tillage instruments, perhaps even smaller versions of existing tractors.

By 1931, Wiman had put Brown and the other engineers to work on new tractor ideas, and a few months later, in April 1932, he sent Brown on a special trip to Dain, Van Brunt, Syracuse, and the Wagon Works to "pep them up somewhat on experimental work." Out of Wiman's constant press for experimental and engineering effort, and his exhortations for fresh ideas, came two new tractors, the Model A (16.22 drawbar horsepower, 23.5 belt-pulley horsepower) and the Model B (9.28 drawbar horsepower, 14.25 belt horsepower). Tested in the Salt River Valley in Arizona in 1933, the Model A was brought into production in the following year; one year later the Model B was introduced.

The two tractors were strikingly successful; both would stay in the product line until 1952, with more than 293,000 of the As sold by that date, more than 309,000 of the Bs. The two tractors rank first and second in popularity over the entire tractor history of the company. The Model A was the solution to Deere's need for a two-plow tractor. Its adjustable wheel tread answered the farmer's need for moving his wheels outward or inward from the then-typical 42-inch standard row. (There had to be this much room for the farm horse to continue to walk on solid ground for each pass through the field.) The implement hitch for the A, as well as the power shaft, was located on the center line of the tractor, substantially reducing any side draft. An industry first, a hydraulic-power lift system increased both the efficiency and speed of operation, as well as providing a "cushion" drop of equipment. There were other important features, for example, a one-piece transmission case that allowed high under-axle clearance.

The simple, powerful two-cylinder engine successfully burned distillate, fuel oil, furnace oil, and similar low-cost fuels, as well as kerosene or gasoline. Thus the engine could be started with gas, then switched over to the lower grade fuels. These cheaper substitutes burned more effectively in the big cylinders of the two-cylinder engines than when used in the conventional four- and six-cylinder engines. This was a period of hard times, and an economical design with economical fuel was particularly important. Wayne Worthington, in his definitive study of the tractor,

A Model B leads the charge in stacking hay.

A Model BN with a mounted beet and bean cultivator, 1938.

evaluated Deere's decision: "Deere & Company had always taken a contrary position with respect to fuels, and as others turned to the use of Regular gasoline (70 octane) they continued to promote the economies made possible by the use of available low cost distillates. A continuing program of combustion research was followed, which resulted in increasing the compression ratio of their distillate burning engines by some 40%. The resulting fuel economy broke existing records when tested at Nebraska. This served to educate tractor users to the importance of fuel economy even though the price of tractor distillate

A wide-front Model BW. (Photographs by Hans Halberstadt)

delivered to the farms was in the order of 8 to 8½ cents per gallon."

The two new tractors were just the right sizes—the Model B was described as "two-thirds the size of the A," and company literature stressed that the A gave the pulling capacity of a six-horse team, the daily work output of from eight to ten horses, with the B having the pulling capacity of a four-horse team and the daily output of six to eight horses. The B was made particularly as a one-plow tractor. It had all the features of the A—the adjustable wheel tread, the clearance, the excellent vision, etc. (and both were available with pneumatic rear tires as alternatives to the regular metal wheels). The B had a hydraulic-power lift and, within a year of their introduction, both were also available with single front wheels (the AN and BN versions). By 1936, there were eleven different versions of the company's three basic tractors—the A, B, and D. Both the A and B were also made with standard tread, there were orchard tractors available (with covered fenders for the rear wheels and no protruding stacks at the top of the tractor), and there were versions of the A and B that had adjustable front-wheel treads, as well as rear-wheel adjustments. As the success of the two new tractors sank in, company literature, such as the catalog of 1936, exultantly extolled the many new features and reaffirmed in aggressive advertising prose the efficacy of the two-cylinder tractor.

Probably no single stage in the entire history of the company's product development was any more important than this one. The appearance of the two new tractors in the depth of the Great Depression was a testimony both to the company's optimism about the future and the farmers' desires for and willingness to buy simple, trouble-free farm tractors. The abiding regard for and love of the two new models—the Model A and the Model B—continued all through the 1930s and '40s up to their final models in 1952 and left a residual of acclaim that made the models collectors' items for tractor buffs down to today.

It is likely that the company would not have taken the steps to initiate these two new models had it not been for Charles Wiman. His longstanding love of both innovation and the engineering to back it up stemmed from his own academic training and his continuing enthusiasm. No armchair philosopher, he was always out in the field observing, and this was seen by everyone to enhance product innovation in the company at a time when it was desperately needed. The expenditures made in that uneasy period were substantial, particularly in light of the cuts in every other expense item in the company, both in factory and branch. It was a gamble by Wiman that was based upon faith and sound judgment, and its payoffs for the company in succeeding years were very great indeed.

Life Down on the Farm in the 1930s

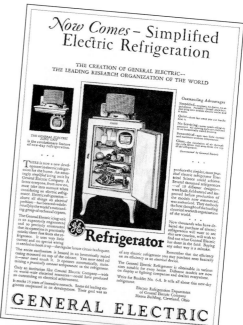

Indoor plumbing and electrification began arriving on farms in the 1930s.

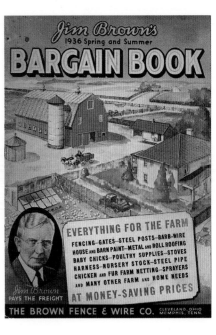

On the Smooth Highway of the Skies

NEW YORK
BOSTON

COLONIAL AIR TRANSPORT INC

Burpee's Bulbs
for FALL PLANTING
1934

Princess Elizabeth

Inglescombe Yellow

Afterglow

Pride of Haarlem

W. Atlee Burpee

ROOSEVELT FOR PRESIDENT

OUR NEXT PRESIDENT
WENDELL LEWIS WILLKIE

CARTER'S Champion Chicks

CARTER'S CHICKERY

GRADE
BOYS AND GIRLS CLUB
RANDOLPH AGRICULTURAL FAIR
RANDOLPH OHIO

GRADE B
BOYS AND GIRLS CLUB
RANDOLPH AGRICULTURAL FAIR
RANDOLPH OHIO
SEPT. 27-28 1935

OYSTER SHELL for POULTRY

SNOW WHITE BRAND

OYSTER SHELL

MANUFACTURED BY
WHITE SHELL CORPORATION
JACKSONVILLE, FLORIDA

Farm Machinery Developments

For Deere's sesquicentennial celebrations in 1937, the two-bottom plows became the Models 4B and 4C while a lighter Model 52 replaced the 40C and 45, and a single-bottom 51 was added. The No. 2 Two-Way tractor plow was introduced in the 1920s and was still in the 1938 full-line catalog; it was available with one- or two-bottoms. The famous Nos. 5 and 6 plows still led the field in the three- to five-bottom class, while the No. 9 Brush-Breaker single furrow was replaced with the No. 11 Integral A-3 and B-3 two-way plows, which were introduced for the new row-crop tractors, a sign of future developments. At the same time, the long, venerable line of horse plows had come to an end.

Disk plows, tillers, and harrows changed little over this period, the chief additions to tillage equipment being integral tools for the row-crop tractors. The famous No. 999 corn planter still held prime position in the planter world

The No. 4 mower replaced the Nos. 1 and 2, and the No. 5 PTO-drive mower was setting new standards and would last in the line until well after World War II. A windrow pick-up press had been added to the hay baler line. Every type of farm equipment was now covered by the company's ever-growing catalog.

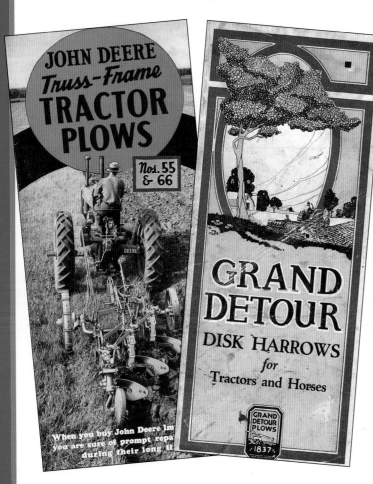

Deere's horse-drawn, one-row potato planter, 1937.

Even when Deere had its own tractors, it still offered implements for the Fordson and other machines, 1923.

Deere's President Charles Wiman with a No. 52 plow, 1936. Wiman served as president from 1928 to 1955.

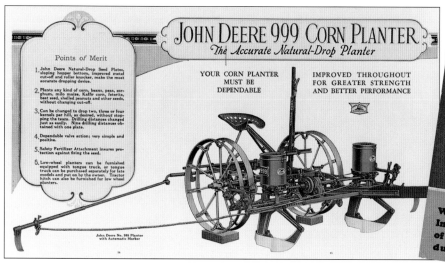

Deere No. 999 corn planter, 1935.

Deere Combines:
The Caterpillar Connection

In the 1880s, in far-off California, a line of combine harvesters was introduced by Benjamin Holt. Built in Stockton, these first link-belt-driven machines were announced in 1886. Some fifty years later in the 1930s, the Holt combines would become part of Deere's full line of farm machinery.

In 1912, Holt purchased its chief rival, the C. L Best Company, adding new combines to the line that now totaled eight different models, including the Baby Special 10- or 12-foot, up to the Large Standard in 18- to 26-foot cut sizes. Also included was the first self-propelled production combine, which was enormously popular and resulted in the production of large numbers of machines. While other combines were of wooden construction, Holt introduced in 1919 the first all-steel combines.

During the 1920s, Deere's combine harvester line was born and developed. Experiments were conducted during 1925–1926 to produce Deere's own design of harvester. In 1927, fifty Model No. 2 combines were built with 12- or 16-foot cuts; they were followed by the No. 1 the next year with optional 8-, 10-, or 12-foot cutter bars. In 1929,

the No. 3 replaced the No. 2, and the No. 5 replaced the No. 1; it was again updated as the 5-A in 1934. An experimental No. 4 Hillside model was built in 1929, but negotiations with Caterpillar to takeover its venerable Holt–Best combine line were taking place, so the No. 4 did not enter production. The large No. 3 was replaced in 1932 with the 17, which was similar but with a 36-inch separator instead of the previous 40-inch.

Deere's answer to the Allis-Chalmers 60 appeared in 1936 as the No. 6 with a similar crosswise threshing mechanism but with a spike-tooth cylinder. It was offered with either PTO or engine drive and on rubber tires. Sadly, it was not a success.

Following the breakdown of earlier negotiations, Deere finally acquired the Caterpillar 36 combine line in 1936. The two smaller Models 34 and 38 were dropped, but the result was a line of level-land and hillside models for both medium and extreme slopes. The Caterpillar-turned-Deere Model 36 combine boasted the longest production run of combine—Twenty-eight years stretching from 1926 to 1951.

Holt's self-propelled harvester, first built in 1911.

Above: *A Vindex model of Deere's combine, 1920s.*

Left: *Model 5A combine brochure.*

Ten horses pull a Holt No. 36 combine.

Deere Combines:
The Caterpillar Connection

A tractor-drawn Holt combine works a hillside, 1930s.

A Johnny Popper pulls a Deere combine, 1930s.

ERE COMBINE

nbine
s *Easier to Operate*

are expert threshermen, you will
ine, features that will meet their
proved mechanical features that
e simplicity of operation that is
farmers who are not experienced
Put the John Deere on display
preference that is bound to grow
abine. Offer your combine pros-

5 Oiling the John Deere is a simple operation that requires
little time. Every bearing can be oiled from the outside of
the machine with a high-pressure grease gun. This high-
pressure system makes thorough oiling a swift and easy job
and longer life results.

6 The motor that operates the John Deere has a surplus of
power, insuring the steady, even speed so essential to good
threshing. It is of four-cylinder type and modern design
throughout.

7 The 65-bushel grain tank on the John Deere is emptied in
less than one minute. This is done by simply turning a
crank that raises two doors at the bottom of the tank. The
saving in time due to this feature alone means many bushels added to the day's run.

apany

The John Deere No. 2 Combine,
shown here, is built in 12- and
16-ft. sizes. Its separator is
24" x 40". The capacity of its
grain tank is 65 bushels.

Deere's No. 2 combine.

Lanz's Expanding Bulldog Line

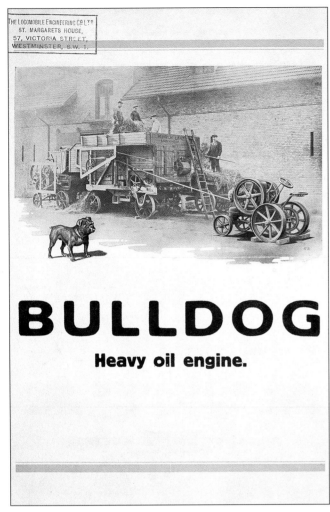

BULLDOG

Heavy oil engine.

Bulldog 12-ps HL brochure.

LANZ

D 3506
Allzweck

20 PS Allzweck-Bulldog

Allzweck-Bulldog D 3506 20-ps brochure.

Why I am the Champion of my Class

Lanz Bulldog Crude Oil Tractor

Bulldog HR4 and HR5 brochure, 1926.

A rare Bulldog HR6 row-crop tractor, 1930. Built in the American style for row-crop machines, it did not catch on with European farmers, and few were built.

Bulldog Series brochure.

Bulldog D 2803 brochure.

Bulldog D 2806 brochure.

Bulldog Series brochure.

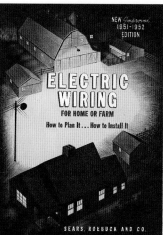

CHAPTER 4

Style Comes to the Farm, 1938–1960

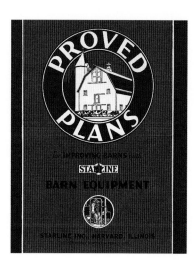

"V for victory" was the symbol as women took to the fields while the men went off to fight in the battlefields of World War II.

Streamlining by Dreyfuss

The biggest change yet in the appearance of Deere's tractors, many of the firm's combines, and other equipment came in 1938. To compete with other companies, Deere hired industrial designer Henry Dreyfuss of New York City to style all its equipment, starting with the Models A and B row-crop tractors; these were followed by the Models D, H, and L tractors the following year. Following Dreyfuss's appointment, it was standard practice to seek his advice on the styling of all new machines where applicable prior to production.

Industrial designer Henry Dreyfuss restyled Deere's tractors, streamlining the bodywork and placing an emphasis on ergonomics that was revolutionary for the day.

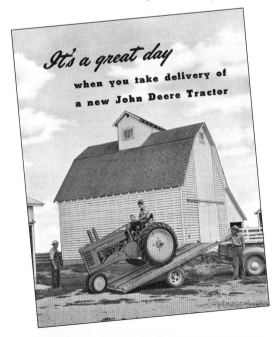

Farm families gathered around the newly styled Deeres at state and country fairs.

TIMELINE

1938: Deere Models A and B receive a styling update from industrial designer Henry Dreyfuss.

1939: Germany invades Poland; France and Great Britain declare war on Germany, sparking World War II. Deere introduces its one-plow Model H. Ford launches its revolutionary lightweight 9N with Harry Ferguson–designed three-point hitch that blaze a trail for modern tractors. First American TV broadcast.

1940: Farmers make up 18 percent of the U.S. labor force with farms averaging 175 acres. 58 percent of U.S. farms have cars; 25 percent have telephones; 33 percent have electricity. Nylon stockings are introduced.

1941: The U.S. enters World War II after the Japanese bomb Pearl Harbor. Deere debuts its Model GM.

1940s: Soybean production expands rapidly in the Corn Belt. First seeded as a drilled crop after small grains in a three-year rotation, soybeans began to become a row crop in the Corn Belt by the end of WWII. The U.S. produces 60 percent of the world's supply of soybeans. Many Corn Belt farms grow primarily corn and soybeans.

1942: First nuclear chain reaction performed, at University of Chicago. T-shirts are introduced.

1944: Allies invade France on D-Day.

1945: Atomic bomb is dropped on Hiroshima, Japan, starting the Nuclear Age. Microwave oven is invented. ENIAC, the first electronic digital computer, sparks the Computer Age.

1946: First meeting is held of the United Nations General Assembly. The bikini bathing suit, created by French couturier Louis Reard, is first modeled by a stripper at a Paris fashion show.

1947: Jackie Robinson breaks the major league baseball color barrier, taking the field with the Brooklyn Dodgers. U.S. Air Force Capt. Chuck Yeager is the first man to exceed the speed of sound. Betty Crocker cake mixes are introduced. Deere buys crawler specialist Lindeman Manufacturing of Yakima, Washington.

1948: The first McDonald's drive-thru restaurant opens, in San Bernardino, California. The transistor is invented.

Streamlining by Dreyfuss

Deere salesman proudly demon-
strate their newly styled Deere
Model A.

The Deeres styled by Dreyfuss were even easier to maintain and work on.

A restored wide-front Model AW.

Above: *A restored narrow-front Model AN. (Photograph by Hans Halberstadt)*

Far left: *Models A and B brochure.*

Left: *Model AR brochure, 1951.*

Wayne Worthington
Johnny Popper Engineer

By Orrin E. Miller

Deere engineer Wayne Harry Worthington was responsible for the design and development of the complete line of John Deere two-cylinder tractors from the Model A of 1934, Model B of 1935, Model G of 1937, Model H of 1938, and Model R of 1948 to the four-wheel-drive 8010 of 1959. His was an auspicious record, stretching from the dawn of the Johnny Popper era to the debut of the New Generation four- and six-cylinder machines.

Wayne was born December 29, 1891, the sole son of James Hiram Worthington and Minnie Belle Barden Worthington. His birthplace was on a farm near Rose Hill, Iowa.

As Wayne grew, his school teachers found him exceptionally bright and industrious. He was skipped from first to fourth grade, then sixth to eighth. His family had moved to Perry, Oklahoma, and he went through Perry High School in three years, graduating in 1907 at age fifteen. In fall 1907, Wayne entered Oklahoma A&M at Stillwater, taking courses in mechanical and electrical engineering. He completed the work in three years and graduated summa cum laude in June 1910, at age eighteen, standing first in his class.

He then went to work for J. I. Case as service manager for Russia and Argentina, working on steam engines and threshers. In 1911, he delivered and assembled the first American gas tractor sold in Russia. While working in Russia, Wayne attended the university in Moscow and took advanced courses in mathematics and dynamics, studying metal strengths and fatigue. In October 1914, the Turkish navy attacked the harbor of Odessa, blowing up Worthington's Case warehouse, so he returned to the United States.

On returning to America he joined the Aultman-Taylor Company in Mansfield, Ohio, as a design and development engineer with a brief to build a thresher suited to Russia. In 1917, he moved to Quincy, Illinois, as chief design and development engineer for the Electric Wheel Company. In 1919, he returned to Aultman-Taylor as chief engineer. While with Aultman-Taylor, he went to the first Nebraska tractor test held in 1920 and was supposed to have been involved in setting the test standards. When Advance-Rumely took over Aultman-Taylor, Wayne became superintendent of the Mansfield, Ohio, plant. In 1924, he moved to Rumely's Battle Creek, Michigan, plant where he became chief engineer and director of engineering. In 1929, he moved to the Gleaner Combine Harvester Company in Independence, Missouri.

In 1930, Wayne moved to Waterloo, Iowa, as a research engineer for Deere's Waterloo Works. He remained with Deere until his retirement in 1959, then worked for the firm as a consultant until his second retirement in 1962.

In his time at Deere, Wayne progressed from research engineer to assistant chief engineer to director of engineering research. He was responsible for the design and development of the Models A, B, G, H, R, and 8010. Deere President William Hewitt wanted the first 8010 built by his birthday, and Wayne finished thirty days ahead of schedule. This tractor justified a new research center to the board of directors in Moline and provided another use for the new six-cylinder engines yet to be introduced in fall 1960.

Wayne was involved in getting rubber tractor tires for farm tractors as early as 1932. He also was involved in putting padding on tractor seats, hydraulics on tractors, and roll-over bars on tractors as a safety feature.

Yet it was Wayne's work on the development of trans-

The Model B received the same styling treatment as the big Model A.

missions that was his great unsung contribution to Deere. Before World War II, Deere had gearbox troubles with its tractors. During the war, Deere developed and produced transmissions for U.S. Army M-3 and M-4 tanks. To do this, Deere established the Iowa Transmission Company in about May 1941 based at its Waterloo Works. Engineering lessons learned in building the bulletproof tank transmissions were subsequently transferred to the tractors following the war. These new gearboxes provided Deere tractors with the least horsepower drop through their transmissions of any farm tractors on the market and were a key reason that Deere machines became the world's leader.

In 1953, Wayne began researching European tractor companies that would be a favorable acquisition for Deere.

He traveled to Germany and Sweden in this pursuit, and finally selected the Lanz firm as it appeared to fit best with Deere's goals of developing a worldwide product line. After Wayne's retirement in 1959, he and his wife lived in Germany for two and a half years organizing the Deere-Lanz works.

In 1957, Wayne cooperated with Pirelli of Milan, Italy, in pioneering and introducing belted tires. In 1959, when Krushchev visited the Deere Works in Des Moines, Wayne gave him the tour since he spoke Russian. By the time of his final retirement in 1962, Wayne was the proud holder of thirty-nine patents.

Wayne Worthington died December 4, 1981, of heart failure.

Above left: *By 1940, Deere's line included eighteen models—although not all were styled yet.*

Above right: *1951 Models A, B, and G brochure.*

An Arcade Deere toy, 1940s.

1950 Model B with Deere 8-foot field cultivator

Electric lights and start had become standard by the time this 1950 Model B rolled off the assembly line of the Waterloo tractor plant. It had the pressed-steel frame common to its model year and a completely enclosed flywheel with the starter placed low in the main gear case. Its six-speed transmission helped the driver adjust the tractor speed to the field need. This improved Model B was a gasoline-burner capable of pulling 24.62 drawbar hp—enough for two-plows under most conditions. The 8-foot spring-tined field cultivator shown here would give the Model B a good workout in heavy soils. Field cultivators are most often used just before planting to work soils into finer particles after moldboard or chisel plowing. Owner: Ken Burden. (Photograph © Ralph W. Sanders)

That Faithful Poppin' Johnny

While Dad eats his lunch, Junior and Spot pretend they are piloting the family's "Poppin' Johnny" in this painting by artist Walter Haskell Hinton.

Deere doll, circa 1940s.

ENJOY GENERAL-PURPOSE TRACTOR PERFORMANCE

at its Best!

WITH
THE RIGHT KIND OF POWER...THE RIGHT AMOUNT OF POWER
FOR YOUR FARM

A little tyke operates the family's styled Model B, 1938.

The Pneumatic Rubber Tire Revolution

Above: *A styled Model D pulls a Deere No. 21 two-row corn picker, 1940.*

Right: *Model D brochure, 1939.*

Opposite page: *Pneumatic rubber tires were one of the greatest advances in tractors in the 1930s, giving rise to cartoons like this about tractor racing.*

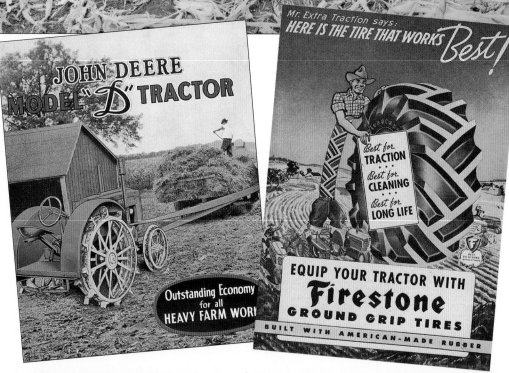

New SPEED FACTOR in Farming

*Low Pressure Tires Promise Possibilities for Expediting
Field Operations Without Increasing Expenditure of Power*

Deere's Iowa Transmission Company

During World War II, Deere developed and produced transmissions for U.S. Army M3 and M4 tanks. To do this, Deere established the Iowa Transmission Company in about May 1941 based at its Waterloo Works.

Before the war, Deere had some gearbox troubles with certain of its tractors. Engineering lessons learned in building the bulletproof tank transmissions were subsequently transferred to the farm tractors following the war. These new gearboxes provided Deere tractors with the least horsepower drop through their transmissions of any farm tractors on the market and were a key reason that Deere machines became the world's leader.

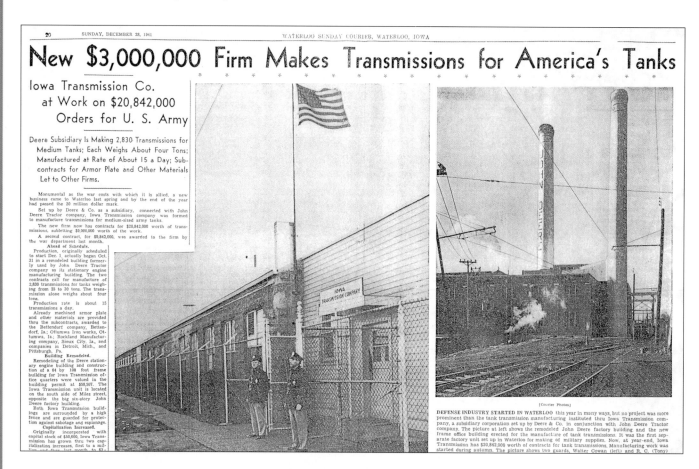

New $3,000,000 Firm Makes Transmissions for America's Tanks

Iowa Transmission Co. at Work on $20,842,000 Orders for U. S. Army

Deere Subsidiary Is Making 2,830 Transmissions for Medium Tanks; Each Weighs About Four Tons; Manufactured at Rate of About 15 a Day; Subcontracts for Armor Plate and Other Materials Let to Other Firms.

Monumental as the war costs with which it is allied, a new business came to Waterloo last spring and by the end of the year had passed the 20 million dollar mark.

Set up by Deere & Co. as a subsidiary, connected with John Deere Tractor company, Iowa Transmission company was formed to manufacture transmissions for medium-sized army tanks.

The new firm now has contracts for $20,842,000 worth of transmissions, subletting $9,000,000 worth of the work.

A second contract, for $9,842,000, was awarded to the firm by the war department last month.

Ahead of Schedule.

Production, originally scheduled to start Dec. 1, actually began Oct. 31 in a remodeled building formerly used by John Deere Tractor company as its stationary engine manufacturing building. The two contracts call for manufacture of 2,830 transmissions for tanks weighing from 25 to 30 tons. The transmission alone weighs about four tons.

Production rate is about 15 transmissions a day.

Already machined armor plate and other materials are provided thru the subcontracts, awarded to the Bettendorf company, Bettendorf, Ia.; Ottumwa Iron works, Ottumwa, Ia.; Rockland Manufacturing company, Sioux City, Ia., and companies in Detroit, Mich., and Pittsburgh, Pa.

Building Remodeled.

Remodeling of the Deere stationary engine building and construction of a 64 by 108 foot frame building for Iowa Transmission office quarters were valued in the building permit at $58,507. The Iowa Transmission unit is located on the south side of Miles street, opposite the big six-story John Deere factory building.

Both Iowa Transmission buildings are surrounded by a high fence and are guarded for protection against sabotage and espionage.

Capitalization Increased.

Originally incorporated with capital stock of $50,000, Iowa Transmission has grown thru two capitalization increases, first to a million and then last month to $3,...

[Courier Photos]

DEFENSE INDUSTRY STARTED IN WATERLOO this year in many ways, but no project was more prominent than the tank transmission manufacturing instituted thru Iowa Transmission company, a subsidiary corporation set up by Deere & Co. in conjunction with John Deere Tractor company. The picture at left shows the remodeled John Deere factory building and the new frame office building erected for the manufacture of tank transmissions. It was the first separate factory unit set up in Waterloo for making of military supplies. Now, at year-end, Iowa Transmission has $20,842,000 worth of contracts for tank transmissions. Manufacturing work was started during autumn. The picture shows two guards, Walter Cowan (left) and R. C. (Tony)...

An M3 tank transmission unit produced by Deere undergoing testing. The original three-piece housing was redesigned as a one-piece unit by Deere engineer Harold L. Brock.

An M3 Sherman on display at Deere with employees lining up for a view of the tank and Deere's transmission.

Fisher ad displaying its armored bodywork for the M3. Deere's transmission was mounted in the front of the tank under the armor plating that's being drawn on.

An M2 tractor as designed by Cletrac with some parts built by Deere. This M2 was one of many assembled in the Deere works. Owner: Albert Duroe.

Farm Living in the 1940s

Farm families had many things to be grateful for in the 1940s.

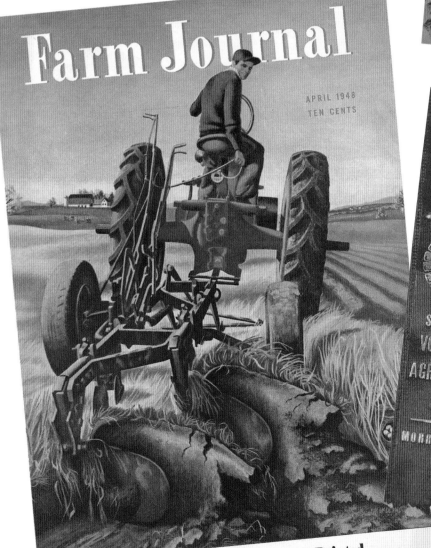

The Big Machine:
Debut of the Model G Series

When the United States entered World War II, wartime restriction went into effect. When the Model G was styled in 1941, the addition of a six-speed gearbox and optional electric starting meant the addition of the letter M for "Modernized," resulting in the Model GM, though the serial number plates still showed Model G.

A Model G pulls a Deere No. 93 disk plow.

A Model G pulls a potato planter, 1938.

Far left: *Model GM leaflet, 1941.*

Left: *Models, G, GM, and GW brochure, 1948.*

A styled Model G, 1940s.

**1938 Model G with
integral G-3 two-way plow**

*Power for larger farms came with the 1937 introduction
of the full three-plow Model G. It was a full four-row
tractor with a big 6.125x7-inch bore-and-stroke engine,
that, when first tested on steel wheels, put out 27.63
drawbar and 35.91 belt hp. When tested in 1947 on
rubber tires, the G's power measured 34.49 and 38.10
hp, respectively. This 1938 Model G is equipped with an
integral 18-inch moldboard two-way plow for level
plowing of flood- or furrow-irrigated land. It drops
alternate bottoms for each plowing pass, turning the soil
in one direction only, to eliminate the lap or dead
furrows made with regular one-way moldboard plows.
The Deere Hydraulic Power-Lift helped the operator
handle heavy four-row implements. Owners: Phyllis and
Wayne Pokorny. (Photograph © Ralph W. Sanders)*

146

World War II and the Fight on the Farm

Deere handbook on keeping machinery alive throughout the war, 1943.

Deere's war-time president, Burton Peek.

"Rosie the Riveter" was at work at Deere, too, as women took over many of the jobs in the company's factories.

The Light-Duty Tractors: Models H, L, LA, and M

Pre-production Model M tractors were at work in 1944–1945, but full production had to await the opening of the new tractor factory early in 1947 at Dubuque, Iowa. Their introduction resulted in the end of the Models L, LA, BR, BO, and the H Series.

The full line of Deere two-cylinder tractors was finally completed with the introduction in the summer of 1948 of the long-awaited diesel Model R, and the similar styling treatment of the last models to be treated, the AR and AO, in 1949. The same year saw the further development of the M Series to include the full row-crop MT Series and the crawler MC to replace the BO-Lindeman.

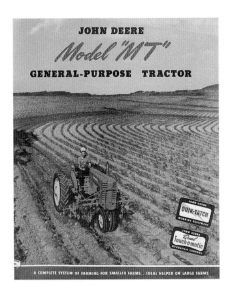

Model MT brochure, 1950.

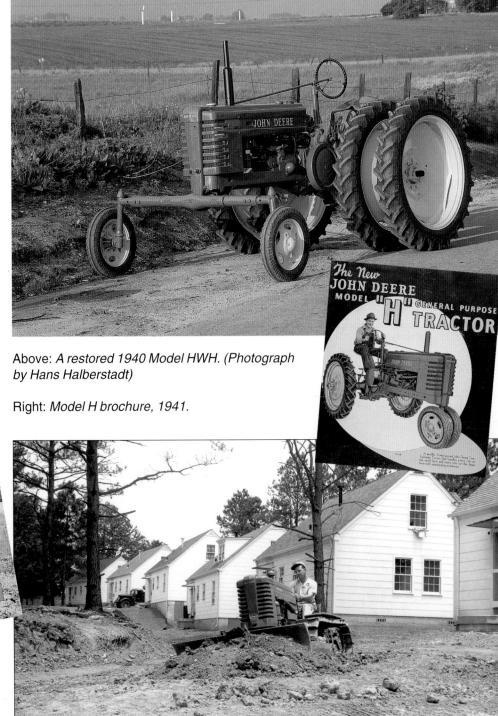

Above: *A restored 1940 Model HWH. (Photograph by Hans Halberstadt)*

Right: *Model H brochure, 1941.*

Above: *Model MC brochure, 1950.*

Right: *A Model MC crawler fitted with a blade, 1949.*

A styled Model L pulls a planter.

An unstyled Model L powers a No. 4 corn sheller.

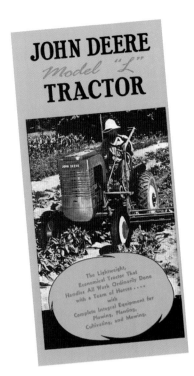

Above: *Models L and LA brochure, 1941.*

Left: *Model LA. (Photograph by Hans Halberstadt)*

Deere's Diesel: Debut of the Model R

Above: *A Model R pulls a Deere grain combine.*

Right: *Model R brochure, 1951.*

Restored Model R. (Photograph by Hans Halberstadt)

The diesel-powered Model R was designed to replace the venerable Model D, but demand for the D kept both machines in the Deere line.

Deere's Tillage and Planting Lines

In tillage and planting, the lines were updated and styled to match the rest of the line with tractor-drawn equipment on rubber tires as standard. This applied also to mowers, rakes, tedders, and other trailed machines. The postwar period saw the gradual withdrawal of sweeps, stackers, hay- and green-crop loaders from the line to be replaced with pick-up balers and forage harvesters. Tractor-mounted loaders—at first rear-mounted but soon transferred to front mounting—became the most common attachment for all but the largest tractors. Initially geared to livestock farming, their usefulness developed into other fields as well.

THE **KEYSTONE** OF MODERN PLOW CONSTRUCTION IS

JOHN DEERE

Truss-Frame Design

JOHN DEERE TRUSS-FRAME PLOWS GIVE YOU
Greater Strength...Clearance...Adaptability

JOHN DEERE
2- AND 4-ROW
QUIK-TATCH CULTIVATORS

FOR JOHN DEERE TRACTORS
MODELS "50," "60," and "70"

FAST, EASY, ONE-MAN
TACHING AND DETACHING
us MANY OUTSTANDING
GOOD-WORK FEATURES

A single-row corn picker mounted on a Model B.

Deere's Implement and Harvesting Lines

Above, both photos: *1950s Deere plowing and haying equipment brochures.*

Right: *Deere added cotton pickers in 1958. This is a self-propelled Model 99, 1960.*

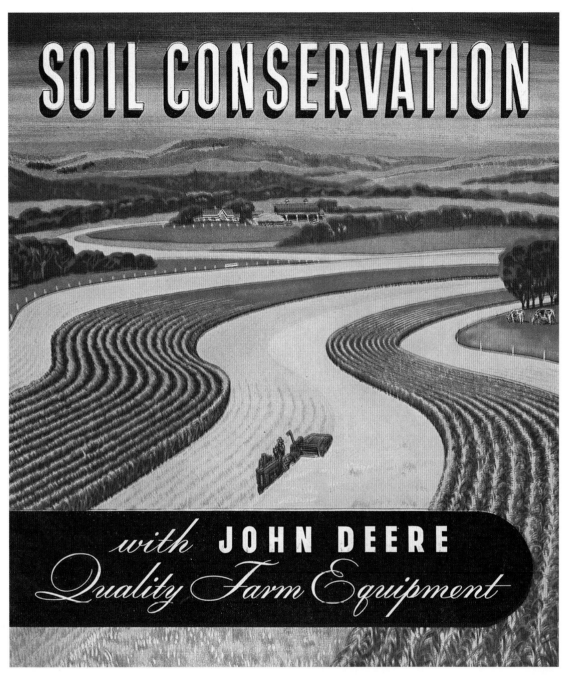

SOIL CONSERVATION

with **JOHN DEERE** *Quality Farm Equipment*

Left: *Deere continued to offer farmers advice on agricultural practices throughout the 1950s.*

Below left: *A Model A powers a Dain hay press baler, 1939.*

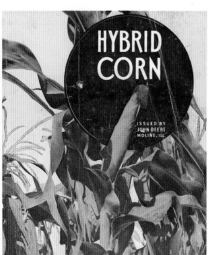

HYBRID CORN

ISSUED BY JOHN DEERE MOLINE, ILL.

Deere promoted the use of corn hybrids—and of course its corn-farming implements.

Deere Combines and Implements

The Nos. 10, 11, and 12 4- through 6-foot-cut combines replaced the No. 6 in 1938 for a short, one-year production run. These were the first combines to receive the a styling treatment. In 1940, the new No. 9 12-foot-cut level-land machine was similarly styled along with its hillside version, the 33. The three small models were changed to left-hand cut the same year, and all subsequent new combine models had similar lines.

The most significant development in the combine harvester world occurred with the introduction in 1947 of Deere's 55 self-propelled combine. Following experiments in 1944–1945, the 55 proved to be the world's most-copied combine, and the original basis of the Claeys/Clayson/New Holland and Claas/Caterpillar machines. From its initial introduction, the 55 was right and needed little of anything other than cosmetic adjustments. From it grew a line of similar machines, the smaller 45, the larger 95 and 105, their hillside equivalents, and the tractor-drawn 42, 65, 96, and 106—a plethora of models that placed Deere as the Number One producer of combines in the world, a position it still retains.

A Model B drives a No. 11 combine, 1939.

A Model B powers a No. 12A combine

The Inside Story of the JOHN DEERE 25

Straight-Through, Full-Width, 6- or 7-Foot COMBINE

cutaway view of the John Deere 25 Straight-Through, Full-Width
mbine shows how the grain and straw are handled from the cutter
ght through the machine.

ground-driven reel, "A," divides the grain and holds it to the cutter
. The cut grain is gently elevated by platform canvas, "C," which,
with feeder, "D," delivers grain in a thin, even stream to the
side rasp-bar cylinder, "E."

e grain travels between cylinder, "E," and concave and open-bar
F," and back against beater behind cylinder, "G," up to 90% of
aration takes place. The grain falls through open-bar grate to shoe
," and is moved back to shoe chaffer—grain is not remixed with
overload straw rack. Beater, "G," deflects grain down through
nt end of the straw rack, and passes the straw onto full-width
ack, "I." Curtains, "H," deflect and retard straw and grain so full
of rack is utilized. During its rearward movement, the remaining
lls through cells in rack onto grain conveyor, "J," and is delivered
shoe pan, "K," which moves it to front end of chaffer. Deflectors
pan, chaffer and shoe sides distribute grain evenly over the en-
aning area. Straw is then tossed out on the ground in a wide,
read.

st of air from fan, "N," is directed by deflector, "O," against shoe
"L," and shoe sieve, "M." This blast, with the aid of chaffer and
itation, blows chaff away and moves the tailings to tailings
P." This auger carries tailings to tailings elevator, "Q," which
them to auger, "R," where they are delivered to the center of the
for re-threshing.

grain, after dropping through shoe chaffer, "L," and shoe sieve,
carried by clean grain auger, "S," to elevator, "T," on opposite
combine and elevated into grain tank.

Successor to the famous No. 12-A

14

15

16

See what goes on inside the

Follow the grain and straw all the way t

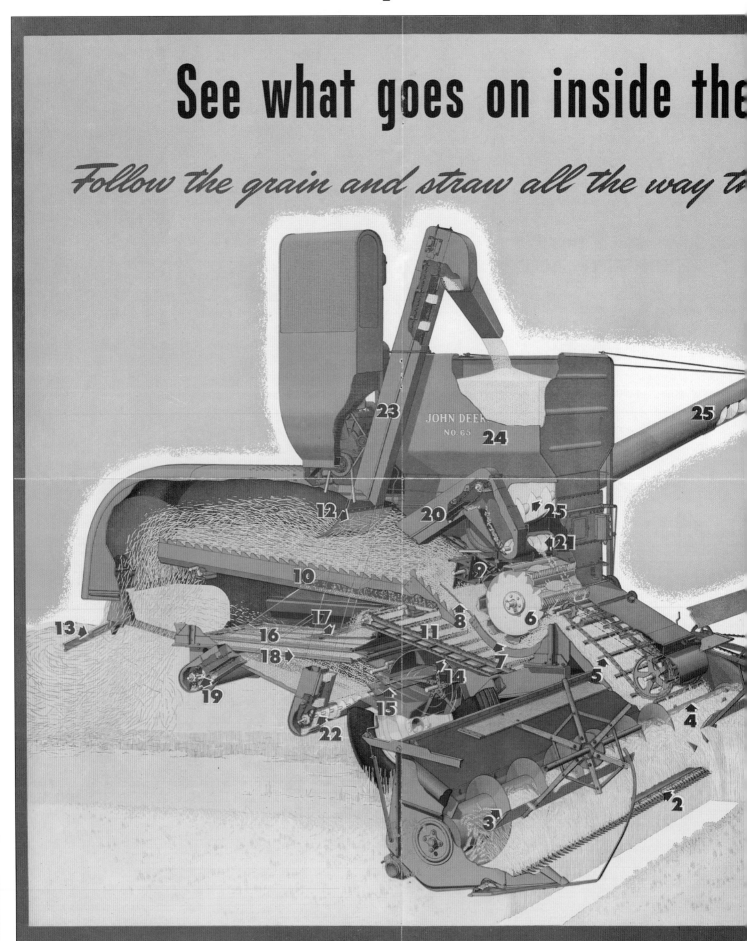

No.65 COMBINE

...ough the machine

THIS CUT-AWAY VIEW of the John Deere No. 65 Combine shows how the grain and straw are handled from the cutter bar on through the machine.

The power-driven reel, 1, divides the grain and holds it to the cutter bar, 2, until cut. The continuous auger, 3, carries the grain to the inner end of the platform. Retracting fingers in auger beater, 4, take the material and feed it positively to the floating, undershot feeder conveyor chain, 5. The feeder conveyor chain, 5, delivers the grain in a steady, positive stream to the extra-large, clean-threshing, rasp-bar cylinder, 6.

As the grain travels between the cylinder, 6, and the concave grate, 7, over grate fingers, 8, and back against the winged separating beater, 9, the greater part of the separating takes place.

Separating beater, 9, strips the straw from the cylinder, deflects the grain through the grate fingers, 8, and passes the straw onto the straw walkers, 10. Up to 90% of the grain falls through concave grate, 7, and fingers, 8, onto conveyor, 11, below cylinder.

Straw and remaining loose grain are passed along to straw walkers, 10. Curtain, 12, keeps grain from being thrown

over. Straw is agitated by straw walkers, 10, on its outward movement and the remaining grain falls through openings in walkers and flows back to conveyor, 11, through grain return pans. Straw is then tossed onto spreader, 13.

After the grain and chaff leave conveyor, 11, a blast of air from undershot fan, 14, through adjustable windboards, 15, is directed against auxiliary chaffer, 17, chaffer, 16, and lower sieve, 18. Blast, with aid of sieve agitation, blows chaff away and moves tailings to tailings auger, 19. This auger carries tailings to tailings elevator, 20, which conveys them through cross-auger, 21, to the center of the cylinder, 6, for re-threshing.

Clean grain, after dropping through auxiliary chaffer, 17, chaffer, 16, and sieve, 18, is carried by clean grain auger, 22, to elevator, 23, which delivers it to grain tank, 24. 25 is grain tank unloading auger.

The self-propelled No. 45 "edible bean" combine, 1957.

The Arrival of the Numbered Series

The tractor nomenclature changed from letters to numbers in 1952, first with the A and B becoming the 60 and 50 respectively, followed by the whole line from the 40 (formerly the M) to the 80, which replaced the R.

A Model 50 picks corn.

1954 Deere Model 60 brochure.

A Model 60 plows a tight corner.

The Arrival of the Numbered Series

A restored Model 60 Orchard. (Photograph by Hans Halberstadt)

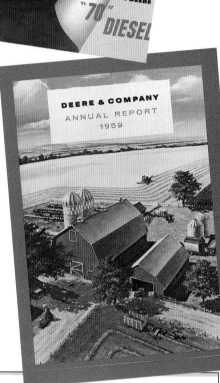

Above: *A Model 70 Hi-Crop diesel row-crop, 1955.*

Right: *Deere's annual report, 1959.*

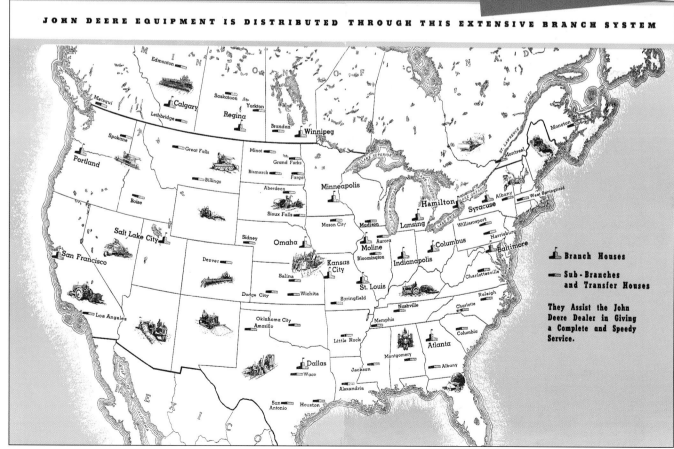

JOHN DEERE EQUIPMENT IS DISTRIBUTED THROUGH THIS EXTENSIVE BRANCH SYSTEM

Branch Houses

Sub-Branches
and Transfer Houses

They Assist the John
Deere Dealer in Giving
a Complete and Speedy
Service.

Deere's branch houses in 1957.

1954 Model 60S LP

This rare 1954 60S LP shown on the edge of an Arkansas rice field (the yellow streak across the upper right is the crop protectant trail laid down by a spray plane), has the high-seat position that marked the later standard tractors. The high seat models were derived from the popular wide-front row-crop models. This three-plow tractor is fitted with rice tires, for extra grip in those soft fields, and it's designed to burn liquefied petroleum or LP-gas, an option first offered by Deere in fall 1953. Only twenty-five tractors of this particular configuration were manufactured. This 60S also features the popular factory-engineered power steering, first offered on the new numbered series Deere models beginning in 1953. Owner: Ford Baldwin. (Photograph © Ralph W. Sanders)

Twenty Percent More Power: The 20 Series

These first numbered models were upgraded in 1955–1956 to the 20 Series of the Models 320 through 820. Except for the new 320 Series, each received about a 20 percent increase in power.

A Model 320 breaks new soil.

Junior liked the feel of the new 20 Series machines.

A Model 420 Crawler shows off its strengths.

A Model 520 works a rotary plow.

A Model 620 Orchard with streamlined protective bodywork.

A Model 720 bails hay.

A Model 820 powers a No. 65 combine.

Farm Living, 1950s Style

Ma and her county-fair blue ribbon get the honors.

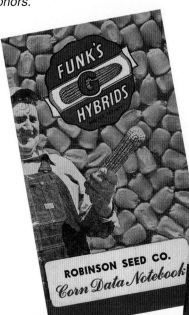

Above: *Tailfins were in—except on farm tractors.*

Left: *Telephone lines were reaching most farms by the 1950s—even if they were still party lines.*

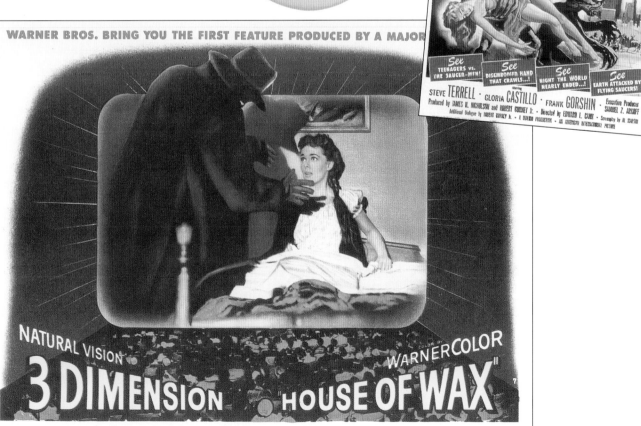

Farm Living, 1950s Style

Prosperity was right around the corner for farm families in the 1950s.

Farm youth started early in their love for Deere tractors.

The Future of the Farmer's Daughter

To the girl on a farm, the war has brought longer hours and harder work.

Help is scarce. The need for crops is greater. There's more and more to be done between sunup and sundown.

The farm girl, like her city cousin, has shouldered her wartime burden willingly. But—more than ever before—her eyes have been opened to the need for electricity and electrical servants in her home.

What is her future to be? The same old drudgery of carrying water and fuel . . . stoking a stove . . . bending over a washboard . . . cleaning lamps . . . pushing a heavy sadiron . . . ?

She dreams of something better. And her dreams can come true, just as they can for the woman in the city. For her home of tomorrow can be a *General Electric* home:

— with hot water—scads of it—always on tap

from a G-E automatic electric water heater . . .

— with a G-E electric range that frees her for other things while the meal practically cooks itself . . .

— with a G-E washer that washes clothes, rinses them, damp-dries them, *all by itself* . . .

— with *everything* electric—from the light on the front porch to the soft, lightweight G-E automatic blanket in the bedroom.

When the war is over, any home within reach of the power line can have these wonders.

General Electric will be making them . . . and developing *new* and even more wondrous appliances to make your life easier and happier.

FOR VICTORY!

Today General Electric is working full speed to hasten the day of Victory.

You can help, too, by buying War Bonds now

"Everything Electrical for After-Victory Homes"

GENERAL ⓖⓔ ELECTRIC

TUNE IN: "The G-E All-Girl Orchestra," Sunday 10 P.M., E.W.T., NBC.—"The World Today" news, every weekday, 6:45 P.M., E.W.T., CBS.

The future looked bright down on the farm.

Many a 4-H youth learned how to maintain the family's tractor from this famous book, Tom Brent and his Tractor. *Naturally, a Deere graced the cover.*

Last of the Johnny Poppers: The 30 Series

In 1958, the 30 Series debuted as basically a styling exercise. It was the last in the long line of two-cylinder tractors.

Above: *A restored Model 830. (Photograph by Chester Peterson Jr.)*

Left: *Model 830 brochure.*

A Model 530 makes hay.

An LPG-fuel Model 430 runs an integral disk harrow .

A Model 630 "harvests" rocks.

A Model 730 Diesel turns soil.

30 Series brochure.

CHAPTER 5

The New Generations, 1959–1991

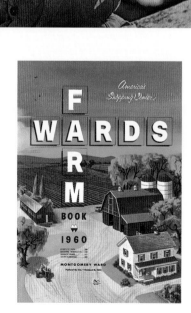

Deere's 3010 and 4010 tractors were landmark machines that would become some of the most copied tractor designs of the 1960s and 1970s. Owner: Kenny Smith. (Photograph by Chester Peterson Jr.)

The Future of the Farm Tractor Arrives

Deere & Company planned the last great display of its 30 Series two-cylinder tractors for September 1959 at Marshalltown, Iowa. Included on the 500-acre site were the new HiLo range of combines and a full line of all the other machines in Deere's catalog. What was not in the catalog was an eight-bottom pickup plow that sat in the middle of a large marquee. The assembled dealers scratched their heads over this implement: What tractor was it designed for?

The answer soon appeared: A four-wheel-drive, 215-hp, GM-engined giant tractor. It bore a strange new number—8-0-1-0, pronounced "Eighty Ten," as the dealers were told. When the outfit made its way to the demonstration area, marshals had to be placed at each end of the field to keep the spectators back as the enormous plow swung round attached to the rear half of the articulated tractor. This amazing machine was a sign of the future for Deere and the rest of the farming world.

The 8010 was unveiled at a Deere field day in autumn 1959.

A rare, restored 8010. Owners: Walter and Bruce Keller. (Photograph by Chester Peterson Jr.)

A lineup of surviving 8010 machines. (Photograph by Chester Peterson Jr.)

The Birth of the Articulated Four-Wheel-Drive Tractor

From the Model 8010 to the Model 7020—and Beyond

By Harold L. Brock

Deere's vice-president of marketing in the 1940s once famously stated that Deere & Company would never need a tractor with more than 50 hp. Yet with the introduction of the New Generation of Deere tractors in 1960, the Model 4010 boasted 80 hp and the Model 5010 was the industry's first tractor exceeding 100 hp when launched in 1963. The times had certainly changed.

The market for the 5010 was predominantly in the large Wheat Belt of the United States and Canada. Farmers teamed the 5010 with large equipment commonly used with crawlers for working at low speeds. The tractor retailed in the $10,000 range, a cost in proportion to the price per horsepower of the Model 4020.

When I joined Deere's engineering research team in 1959, Wayne Worthington and his crew were exploring the feasibility of producing a tractor similar to the heavy-duty Wagner made by the Wagner Tractor Company of Portland, Oregon. The Wagners were large, four-wheel-drive units marketed in the Wheat Belt of the Pacific Northwest and offering competition to the big Caterpillar tractors. At this time, Deere & Company had many combination Deere-Caterpillar dealers in the Northwest: Deere furnished the large implements that farmers required for their Cat crawlers.

Feasibility studies indicated that Deere could produce a similar-sized tractor to the Wagner at approximately the same retail price. Wagner purchased the majority of components from outsources and fabricated its own frame chassis and sheet metal. Deere design objectives included a similar approach to limit investment capital and sample the market. The product was designed with many new features. Component suppliers to Wagner were contacted for their recommendations. Experimental vehicles were built and tested to determine functional feasibility. Deere

management agreed to produce 100 tractors to test the market. Most of these Model 8010 machines went to the Pacific Northwest and only a few were sold east of the Mississippi River.

Yet Deere's cost for the purchased components in the 8010 resulted in a retail price of approximately $30,000. This was a substantial increase over the Model 5010, but then the power was also doubled. Still, in the end, the price range limited sales and the program was eventually canceled.

Several years after the introduction of the Model 8010 and 5010, a four-wheel-drive tractor was introduced for the Wheat Belt by Versatile Manufacturing of Winnipeg, Manitoba. Yet Versatile had limited resources and organization. Their true costs were apparently not known as the product retailed for approximately $13,000.

As the retail cost of the Model 5010 started to approach that of the Versatile tractor, Deere was challenged to offer a competitive four-wheel-drive tractor exceeding the 121 hp of the 5010. It was decided that the best way to approach this competition was to develop a product using as many high-production current tractor parts as possible. This was accomplished by bisecting the larger two-wheel-drive tractor and using available components in production. An articulated chassis design was developed that could be retailed in a price range of the Versatile unit. This new Deere Model 7020 established a standard of performance for Wheat Belt and heavy-tillage operations and formed the basis of future larger models as the market progressed in size and price.

The market had not been ready for the gigantic jump in price between the 5010 and 8010 models. But with the Model 7020, Deere hit the mark—and set the style for the future of large, articulated, four-wheel-drive tractors.

Deere 7020. (Photograph by Chester Peterson Jr.)

Deere updated the 8010 as the 8020 in 1965, but the massive articulated tractor was still ahead of its time. Owner: Jeff McManus. (Photograph by Chester Peterson Jr.)

The 8010 was big. It stood more than 8 feet tall and weighed 25,000 pounds.

Deere contracted with the Wagner Tractor Company of Portland, Oregon, to build the 225-hp WA-14 and 280-hp turbo WA-17. The Wagners filled the slot until Deere had its 7020 and 7520 ready for the market in 1970.

7020 and 7520 brochure.

Deere 7520. (Photograph by Chester Peterson Jr.)

TIMELINE

1959: Deere introduces is radical high-horsepower, four-wheel-drive, articulated Model 8010, heralding the demise of the two-cylinder Deere tractor and the dawn of a new age of high-horsepower tractors. Deere updates its other tractors as the Thirty Series. Alaska and Hawaii are admitted as the 49th and 50th states. Fidel Castro takes over Cuba. The first computer chip is patented.

1960: On D-Day, August 29, Deere launches its New Generation of Power tractors and implements, marking the end of the two-cylinder Johnny Popper and the dawn of the modern Deere tractor powered by tradition-breaking four- and six-cylinder engines. Farmers make up 8.3 percent of the U.S. labor force with farms averaging 303 acres. One U.S. farmer supplies food for 25.8 persons in the U.S. and abroad. 96 percent of U.S. corn acreage planted with hybrid seeds. Francis Gary Powers is shot down in U-2 spy plane over Russia. John F. Kennedy elected U.S. president. First laser is operated.

1962: Deere launches its flagship Model 5010 with 121 hp. John Glenn becomes the first American to orbit the earth.

1963: John F. Kennedy is assassinated in Dallas; Vice-President Lyndon B. Johnson becomes president. Deere enters the lawn and garden field with its Model 110. Betty Friedan publishes *The Feminine Mystique*. Martin Luther King Jr. makes his "I Have a Dream" speech. More than 15,000 U.S. soldiers are in Vietnam by year's end.

1964: The Canadian maple leaf flag replaces the Red Ensign. Ford debuts Mustang "pony car." The Hell's Angels are catapulted into the national spotlight following a wild beach party near Big Sur, California. Hasbro launches its GI Joe.

1965: 5 labor-hours are required to produce 100 bushels of wheat with tractor, 12-foot plow, 14-foot drill, 14-foot self-propelled combine, and trucks. Civil rights unrest reaches a peak in Selma, Alabama. Malcom X is assassinated.

1966: First artificial heart is implanted in a human.

1967: Canada celebrates its Centennial Year, marking the 100th anniversary of Confederation. First football Super Bowl.

1968: Martin Luther King Jr. is assassinated. 83 percent of U.S. farms have phones; 98.4 percent have electricity.

1969: The Concorde makes its first flight. Neil Armstrong is the first man to walk on the moon. Richard M. Nixon becomes U.S. president. *Sesame Street* first airs on TV.

1970: Deere launches its Model 7020, the successor to the Models 8010 and 8020 in the high-horsepower, four-wheel-drive, articulated tractor field. Deere purchases Chamberlain Industries, Australia's largest builder of farm tractors. Farmers make up 4.6 percent of the U.S. labor force with farms averaging 390 acres. No-tillage agriculture is popularized. The Nobel Peace Prize is awarded to Norman Borlaug for developing high-yielding wheat varieties.

D-Day: The New Generation Makes Its Debut

In August 1960, the New Generation of Deere tractors was born. Some 6,000 dealers were flown to Dallas, Texas, to witness this revolution. With this one move, the firm jumped ten years ahead of the opposition. With its advanced tractor and combine lines, Deere & Company became the world's Number One farm machinery manufacturer in 1963—a position it has long retained.

The New Generation was unveiled in Dallas, Texas, on August 29, 1960, before more than 6,000 dealers.

3010 and 4010 brochure.

This cutaway show 4010 provided a welcome anatomy lesson in the advances heralded by the tractor. (Photograph by Chester Peterson Jr.)

Engineering the New Generation

By Harold L. Brock

As early as 1953, Deere & Company management mandated its engineers to begin work on an all-new generation of farm tractors to replace the venerable, beloved two-cylinder Johnny Poppers. The engineering and development of the New Generation of Power was so thorough and so complete that it was not until 1960—seven full years later—that they were launched.

Tractor design has been both revolutionary and evolutionary. A few major designs have advanced the state of the art. Most noteworthy and unique have been Henry Ford's Fordson tractor with its unitized chassis and low cost; International Harvester's tricycle general-purpose row-crop Farmall; and the Ford-Ferguson 9N with its three-point hitch that established the chassis configuration used on all tractors produced today.

At the same time, farming practices continued to change with the advances occurring in plant science, development of herbicides and insecticides, and use of chemical fertilizer. These factors had to be taken into consideration in the design of a new tractor configuration.

Deere's New Generation tractors incorporated the many new advances of the industry and took the state of the art of tractor design to a much higher level than competitors by incorporating unique approaches to operator comfort and control. These models were developed from a clean sheet of paper and not the typical updating of older models. The main carryover from the previous models was the color—green and yellow, of course. With all-new parts, a major retooling and reprocessing of manufacturing resources also became necessary. This major undertaking was one key reason for extending the program timing from 1953 to 1960.

Engineering feasibility studies commenced in 1953 to establish the features and functional concepts to be incorporated in the new 3010 and 4010 models of tractors. Extensive research was carried out to determine horsepower requirements associated with increased operating speeds. Increased tillage travel speeds were becoming more important to improve operational efficiency and flexibility. Concepts of new powertrains and operator stations and controls were investigated. Henry Dreyfuss's industrial design organization was involved in styling and operator comfort considerations. Incorporating the three-point-hitch concept for mounting implements permitted moving the operator ahead of the rear axle. Moving the operator forward and lower permitted improved ride and safety.

A steering committee was organized and a few engineers, under the direction of Merlin Hansen, explored the most satisfactory approach to accomplish the objectives. This activity was isolated from the Deere factory for security reasons. As the program progressed, it was determined that an all-new product engineering facility should be established under the management of Deere instead of the local factory.

This was a wise decision because of the magnitude of the program and its effect upon sister factories and future worldwide product planning objectives of the corporation. This corporate decision was a milestone in determining the future success of Deere & Company. Charles Deere Wiman and his seasoned management team turned the reigns over to new president William Hewitt in 1955 with the challenge of how best to develop Deere into a worldwide industry leader. This brought about new creative thinking and broadened the scope of corporate planning.

A restored 4010. (Photograph by Chester Peterson Jr.)

John Deere formed his company based upon his most successful plow. He and his successors then broadened the product line by joining forces or acquiring various successful smaller companies, such as the Waterloo Gasoline Engine Company and its Waterloo Boy tractor as well as various smaller implement and equipment companies. Corporate philosophy determined that these smaller companies should be kept as independent of corporate control as feasible in order to assure they concentrated on their market. Management objectives stressed decision making at the lowest level.

Establishing a new product engineering center answering to corporate headquarters provided greater emphasis on cooperation with all sister factories for compatibility of the tractors and implements. The Waterloo product engineering center worked closely with the tractor factory and Deere implement and equipment engineers to assure the new generation of tractors fulfilled corporate objectives.

While chief engineer of the Ford tractor operations in 1957, I had the pleasure of visiting Merlin Hansen at the new John Deere Research Engineering center in Waterloo, Iowa. I was most impressed with the new facility and his staff. Little did I know that I would be joining the activity in 1959 as a result of being fired by Ford Motor Company. I had refused to put into production a power-shift transmission that was doomed to failure. The developer of this transmission was a close associate of the new Ford management and misled them to believe this product was ready for production. I suggested that if they wanted to put the product into production they should obtain a new chief engineer. This they did. The promoter of the transmission took my place and was later fired along with his tractor divisional manager because the product was a complete failure and shut the factory down. I mention this because when I joined Deere in 1959, Deere management was concerned that Ford would have a power-shift transmission and the New Generation of tractors would not have this feature. I assured them that Ford would not be a threat and our group would develop an outstanding transmission for the subsequent Models 3020 and 4020.

Upon my arrival at Deere, the New Generation of tractors were in its final stages of development and test to assure the product met Deere's high standards of durability and reliability. My assignment was to assist the research group in the advanced designs of tractors and components. The design of a power-shift transmission was commenced as well as feasibility studies associated with producing a large four-wheel-drive tractor similar to the Wagner and later launched as the Model 8010.

The final design of the New Generation of tractors incorporated many new features for Deere. More importantly, components design brought new advances not offered in the industry.

John Deere's Waterloo and Dubuque tractors were often known as "Johnny Poppers" because of the recognizable combustion sound different from all other tractor makes. With the New Generation, inline four- and six-cylinder engines having many common parts replaced these low-speed two-cylinder engines. The new design provided a narrower engine for better visibility and more flexible operating characteristics. The range of the engine's operating speed was increased providing greater flexibility. We considered the concern farmers might have when changing from a low-speed-sounding engine to a higher-rpm engine. However, the piston speed of the higher-rpm engine was not increased in order to provide the same long life as the old Johnny Poppers. As customers eventually found, the higher-speed engines offered greater flexibility in addition to long life, and the concern never developed.

With a broadened engine range it was determined that additional speeds should be available. An eight-speed synchromesh transmission added required travel options and ease of shifting versus the older clash-shift transmission. Placing controls on the dash permitted comfortable operation when sitting or standing.

A double-reduction planetary-design rear axle was incorporated to reduce the chassis length and to overcome the problem of large final-drive gear tooth contact changing as the rear axleshaft deflected from the drive load. Dry brakes, subject to outside effects and possible leaking seals, were replaced by internally cooled wet brakes.

With ever-increasing manual efforts to control the vehicle and implements, a unique hydraulic system was devised to provide power to multiple sources upon demand. All of the industry's tractors contained simple, open-center hydraulic systems except the Ford tractor with its closed-center single-circuit design for the three-point hitch. The disadvantages of the open-center circuit with the pump running at full volume when not on demand was overcome by Deere's closed-center variable-volume constant-pressure pump that stroked back to neutral when not in demand yet responded to multiple circuit demands. This was an advance over the Ford tractor's simple circuit and the limitations of the open-circuit design of competitors. Deere's unique design permitted hydraulic power availability to multiple uses such as power braking, steering, implement control, and so on. This was very advanced in respect to the industry.

Henry Dreyfuss & Associates had been assisting Deere in industrial design since the styling of the two-cylinder tractors. The firm now became a major player in the New Generation and in improving the corporate image under William Hewitt. The Dreyfuss staff worked closely with

A 3010 powers a No. 30 soybean combine.

A restored 3010. (Photograph by Chester Peterson Jr.)

A restored 1010. (Photograph by Chester Peterson Jr.)

An Ertl 4010 Diesel toy model.

the project engineers to make the designs attractive and ergonomically acceptable to the user. Their close working relationship with the engineers provided a critique thus assuring attractiveness and balance. Several tractor chassis configurations were developed before finalizing the chassis concept. Functional objectives of vision, ergonomic controls, and operator comfort played a major role in the final decision. Proportion and balance were finally obtained.

The new concept of tractor design involved providing a tractor that could be operated by a wide range of ages and sizes. Operator seating and controls became a major consideration. Dreyfuss & Associates brought in orthopedic specialist Dr. Janet Travell to assist the product engineers in this area of concern. Dr. Travell was known for her work with the President John F. Kennedy in treating his back problems. At Deere, she became key in the design of a new concept of seating. Various densities of foam rubber and their shape and location were specified to eliminate pressure points in supporting the operator. This development established a new standard for seating comfort. For generations, the industry had used a steel pan seat form with limited suspension. Because many farmers had back problems due to lifting and aging, seating comfort was an appealing new feature. The new tractor chassis also located the operator nearer the center of gravity of the vehicle, which resulted in less pitching and tossing of the operator station.

With the operator properly positioned, location of the control mechanisms were established to provide ease of operation with minimum effort. With hydraulic power assist, this reduced operator fatigue associated with a long day in the saddle. The shape of the controls were established to provide pleasant form and identification, an approach found desirable in aircraft operator controls.

The overall shape and form of the tractors' sheet metal enhanced the appearance of the machines. Many tractor competitors used simple sheet metal bending to save cost. With die-formed shapes, Deere's styling now reflected highlights and pleasant contours.

With the introduction of the Waterloo-built Models 3010 and 4010 in 1960, Deere was also producing two smaller-horsepower utility tractors in Dubuque, Iowa, and another series of smaller tractors in Mannheim, Germany. The Dubuque tractor and Lanz design components and features had no common design and were also different from the 3010 and 4010 Series. However, New Generation styling was incorporated in these tractors to identify them as part of the Deere family of products, and they were termed the 10 Series. These tractors were updated in the 20 Series to contain common features and designs contained in the 3010 and 4010 Series. The advantages were enormous.

The magnitude of the New Generation of tractors and equipment was apparent to all when they were introduced to the dealer organization and press in Dallas, Texas. Acceptance was encouraging; however, time would prove if the customer accepted this all-new lineup.

With higher horsepower and more flexible speeds, field operations and equipment would have to be matched to take advantage of the increased power. The previous heavier, slower-speed tractors were being replaced by lighter, more-nimble machines. The new series of tractors was intended to work at higher speeds with less drawbar pull. Early in the program, reports were surfacing that many farmers wanted to use current equipment that they pulled at low speeds. The newer, higher-horsepower tractors in some cases could not pull as much as the previous heavier, low-horsepower models. These objections were overcome by excessive ballasting of the newer models. Fortunately, the tractors were designed conservatively and could handle the additional weight. As with any new concept of design and operation, it took a few years for the customers to recognize the advantages of the all-new designs. Feedback from the operators throughout North America was most helpful in updating the design to the 3020 and 4020 Series. Built-in additional weight was included in the 20 Series as well as a new power-shift transmission option.

Merlin Hansen, who had done such a marvelous job of heading up the 3010 and 4010 tractors, unfortunately had a serious heart attack in 1962. Deere management then gave me the opportunity to head the worldwide tractor design operations. Because of my twenty-eight years of experience with Ford, the success of the Ford N tractor, and its revolutionary three-point hitch, Deere believed I was qualified to head up the engineering activity. I had worked with the talented Deere engineers for several years, and we agreed that the challenge of becoming a worldwide leader in the industry was a true opportunity that could be accomplished.

With my arrival at Deere and the subsequent failure of Ford's power-shift transmission, a program was started to design a heavy-duty power-shift transmission. Kenneth Harris did the design work and James Jensen the development work with the objective of having it in production in the 3020 and 4020 Series. Deere purchased two of the Ford tractors with power-shift transmissions. Under test, both failed in a few hours. Deere's design goals stressed a long life under heavy-duty conditions. Experimental samples were field-tested under abnormal conditions that would destroy parts until we got things right. The design proved structurally sound, and production samples were built and underwent similar tests with success. In order to assure Deere would not have field problems with the customer, 100 transmissions were built and sold, and engineers followed up to assure no problems were discovered. The program was successful, and the design swung into full production for the 3020 and 4020.

During the early 1960s, Waterloo product engineering was involved in designing industrial tractors before the industrial division of engineering was established at the Dubuque factory. Tractors with loaders were tested under extreme operating conditions with high elevated loads and rapid maneuvering. Under such a test operation, one of the operators was crushed by tractor overturn. A program was immediately started to provide a roll-guard structure for such test operations. The only base available involved four poster structures used in forestry operations. So, a two-poster design was developed to provide ready access to the operator station and compatibility with mounted equipment. Samples were built and a mannequin—nicknamed Sam the Simulated Man—obtained to provide data relating to damage to the operator. In rolling the tractor off an incline, the proper structure was developed to withstand the impact. Sam the Simulated Man was instrumental in determining how a human might be hurt by the impact of a rollover.

Deere & Company always shared with competitors safety developments, and we now believed the Roll-Gard development fell in this category of importance. The competition was invited to our Research Engineering center to observe a tractor being rolled over an embankment. It was a sub-zero day and the ground was frozen. While we had rolled the tractor successfully many times, the ground had been soft and temperatures more mild. This day the unit failed because the hardware holding the Roll-Gard to the tractor was temperature sensitive. Upon correcting this, we encouraged other tractor manufacturers to start similar development programs and Deere would share

ANNOUNCING A NEW **117 H.P.** TRACTOR!

5010 brochure.

knowledge to help. This roll-testing of tractors was most helpful in the subsequent design of roll structures for enclosed cabs.

During my watch over Deere tractor engineering involving the 3020, 4020, and subsequent models, the development of the industry's first deluxe cab was essential in positioning Deere as a true leader. It was exciting development work.

Prior to Deere's cab program, various manufacturers produced aftermarket cabs in order to get the operator out of the weather and dust. These units were costly and uncomfortable because of noise, heat, and dust. As several of the cabs were being sold for large Wheat Belt tractors, Deere was aware of the need for more operator comfort. Tests were underway in the early 1960s to solve the problem. Air-conditioning and noise-suppression test data was obtained to help future developments. With the introduction of the Roll-Gard structure by Deere, more emphasis was made to design a cab that provided comfort and was competitive to the aftermarket cabs offered by independents. Design concept criteria was established stating that the cab would be an isolated pod to eliminate vibration and noise and the cost should be competitive.

The automobile industry had done limited work in sound suppression in cars and trucks so contacts with the major car engineers was of little help. However, we obtained the name of an acoustical engineer in New York City. This man had experience in building design and vibration-induced noise. He was brought to the Research Engineering center to help address the problems. With his help, James Jensen and others at Deere became students of a new art. Vibration modes of the chassis were determined, and the most advantageous mounting location of the cab was determined. Rubber isolation was incorporated to free the cab of vibration. Because the complete cab was to be isolated from the chassis, all controls, including the steering mechanisms, brakes, clutches, and so on, were a part of the cab to free transmission of noise and vibration. This concept obviously eliminated aftermarket cabs being offered competitively.

Having reached satisfactory noise levels within the cab, we moved on to the much more difficult challenge of developing the air control for comfort. Unlike in cars, the styling of the cab for vision and operator control required large areas of glass. This required extra-capacity air-conditioning for comfort. The only air-conditioning compressor on the market for the car industry was the York used by Ford and the Delco used on General Motors cars. Of the two, the Delco was the most attractive due to its shape and capacity. Deere engineers thus wanted to use this unit for development. When Deere purchasing requested GM to sell the compressor to them, Delco indicated it made millions of units, all the same, and would not consider

A 4010 Diesel harvest beets.

selling to someone who might want changes to the unit. The GM Delco factory manager happened to be on a Society of Automotive Engineers committee with me, and so I convinced him that his operation probably lost more units each day than Deere would need, and under scouts honor, Deere would not ask for changes. When he agreed to my plea, Deere engineers started field-testing.

Because the tractor had no suspension and exposed the compressor to greater dust, heat, and vibration compared to cars, the front seal and bearing had limited life. The engineers developed a dust, heat, and vibration box and worked with the bearing and seal suppliers to solve the problem. This was a real challenge as the changes would have to fit in the limited space available and not increase the cost of the unit. Upon satisfactory completion of the tests, I had the humble experience of telling my friend that my scouts honor pledge had to be broken. The good news was that the changes proposed were minimal, and the compressor would be satisfactory should they

ever consider selling to others in the industrial field. This proves that engineering and politics have to be bedfellows at times.

After satisfactory completion of the cab development, management asked Deere's Marketing Manager Lyle Cherry how many tractors he could sell. As 10 percent of Wheat Belt tractors were being fitted with aftermarket cabs, he projected Deere could increase sales at least 15 percent. Because of the great pent-up demand for a comfortable, quiet, air-conditioned cab, the market demand advanced to 50 percent. Demand continued to increase faster than Deere could increase production facilities.

Today, practically all tractors are offered with cabs. It is noteworthy that Deere was the leader of the industry in introducing a quiet, comfortable, air-conditioned cabin. It took several years for the competition to copy the concept. The cab added 25 percent to the capacity of the factory and was the feature that made the Model 4020 one of the most popular tractors ever produced.

The Rusty Palace:
A New Home for Deere & Company

William Hewitt became Deere & Company president in 1955. He was the son-in-law of Charles Deere Wiman, and oversaw the debut of the New Generation tractors. He served as president from 1955 to 1964 and chairman from 1964 to 1982.

President William Hewitt, left, and famed architect Eero Saarinen examine a model for the new Deere headquarters building, 1960.

TIMELINE

1972: Deere Generation II tractors are unveiled on August 19 with innovative Sound-Gard bodies featuring revolutionary safety and comfort. Five men are arrested for break-in at Democratic headquarters in Watergate offices. Pocket calculators are introduced.

1973: Deere celebrates 50 years of building tractors. Last U.S. troops leave Vietnam.

1973: OPEC oil embargo causes fuel shortages.

1974: Evel Knievel attempts to jump Idaho's Snake River Canyon with his jet-powered "SkyCycle." Nixon resigns; Vice-President Gerald Ford becomes president.

1975: 90 percent of U.S. farms have phones; 98.6 percent have electricity. 3¾ labor-hours are required to produce 100 bushels of wheat with tractor, 30-foot sweep disk, 27-foot drill, 22-foot self-propelled combine, and trucks. 3⅓ labor-hours are required to produce 100 bushels of corn with tractor, five-bottom plow, 20-foot tandem disk, planter, 20-foot herbicide applicator, 12-foot self-propelled combine, and trucks.

1976: Jimmy Carter is elected U.S. president.

1978: First test-tube baby is born.

1979: Shah of Iran is overthrown by Islamic fundamentalists led by Ayatollah Khomeni; 90 hostages are taken. Nuclear accident at Three Mile Island. Sony introduces the Walkman. Margaret Thatcher is elected first woman prime minister of Great Britain.

1980: Farmers make up 3.4 percent of the U.S. labor force with farms averaging 426 acres. Ronald Reagan elected U.S. president.

1981: IBM debuts its personal computer. AIDS is identified.

1982: Robert A. Hanson is named Deere CEO. Space shuttle *Columbia* completes its first flight.

1985: Mikhail Gorbachev calls for glasnost and perestroika.

1986: Major accident at Soviet nuclear plant at Chernobyl.

1987: 3 labor-hours are required to produce 100 bushels of wheat with tractor, 35-foot sweep disk, 30-foot drill, 25-foot self-propelled combine, and trucks. 2¾ labor-hours are required to produce 100 bushels of corn with tractor, five-bottom plow, 25-foot tandem disk, planter, 25-foot herbicide applicator, 15-foot self-propelled combine, and trucks. U.S. farmland values bottom out.

1987: Deere celebrates its 150th anniversary. Dow-Jones Industrial Average drops 508 points in one day in the worst stock market crash in history.

1988: Scientists warn that global warming may affect the future viability of American farming.

1989: More farmers begin to use low-input sustainable agriculture (LISA) techniques to decrease chemical applications. The Berlin Wall falls, signifying the end of Soviet communism. George Bush becomes U.S. president.

1990: Hans W. Becherer is elected Deere chairman.

Above and facing page: *Eero Saarinen's gorgeous headquarters for Deere & Company was affectionately nicknamed "The Rusty Palace" because of the use of corrosion-limited steel beams. The first offices were occupied in 1964.*

Lanz: Joining Forces across the Ocean

The 200,000th Bulldog rolled off the lines in 1956 when Deere bought out Lanz and continued to build a long list of tractors at the famed Mannheim, Germany, works through to the present. The Mannheim-made Deeres continue to be sold around the globe as well as being imported into the United States.

Bulldog D 5016 flyer.

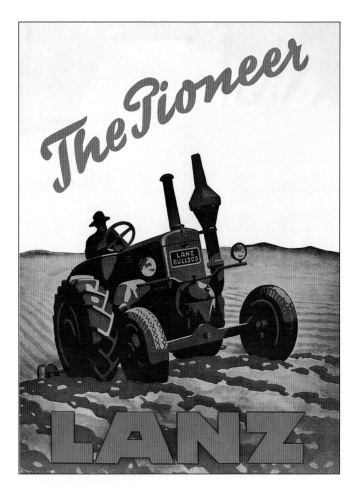

Lanz Bulldog brochure.

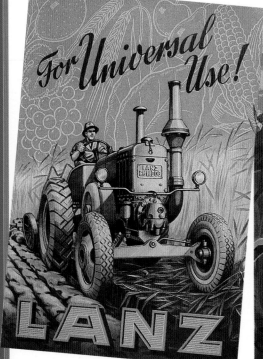

Bulldog D Series brochure, 1950.   *Bulldog D 2206 and D2806 Series brochure.*

Bulldog D 9500 Series cutaway drawing.

Bulldog D 2206 leaflet, 1952.

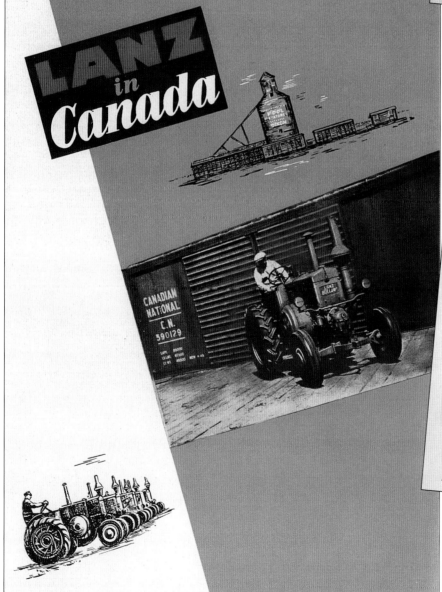

Bulldog D 5506 brochure.

Canadian Bulldog brochure, 1950s.

Deere Tractor Developments

In January 1960, the Mannheim factory introduced two new tractors ahead of the Dallas announcement, the 300 and 500 along with the still-to-be-announced 1010 engine from Dubuque. Followed in 1962 by a two-cylinder 100 and a larger 700 with the 2010 engine, these four models were updated in 1966 as the Ten Series of the 200, 310, 510, and 710 with Dubuque-designed engines built in a new factory at Saran, near Orléans in France.

John Deere Lanz 100, 300 and 500 tractors outside the Mannheim works, 1960.

100 brochure.

Assembling tractors at Mannheim.

10 Series brochure.

700 brochure.

300 tractor in the United States. (Photograph by Chester Peterson Jr.)

Farm Living in the 1960s and 1970s

A Rilco barn with prefab joists is erected by the farmer and seven neighbors in just seven hours, 1960.

Lawn and Garden Tractors: A Farm Tractor for the City

Deere soon branched into all sorts of home-care power equipment, from walking and riding mowers to snowblowers.

MATCHED WORKING EQUIPMENT FOR JOHN DEERE LAWN AND GARDEN TRACTORS

Deere debuted its AMT in 1987.

See the **NEW JOHN DEERE**
110 Lawn and Garden Tractor

Try its exclusive Independent
ground-speed control

RICHARD H. ENNIS INC.
Burrville, N.Y.
P. O. Star Route, Watertown, N.Y.

Tractor about 675.00

Outstanding Features:

7 h.p. 4-cycle engine
Ignition key (neutral gear) safety starter
Fiber glass hood and fenders
Brakes both rear wheels
Turns outside a 28-inch-radius circle
Adjustable rear-wheel tread . . . 27 or 33 inches

Exclusive 3-way ground-speed control . . .
3 speeds forward, one reverse in 7 speed ranges . . . on-the-go
speed change controlled by clutch pedal, speed-control lever, and throttle

Above: *Deere entered the lawn and garden tractor market in 1963 with its 110. The success of this tractor opened a burgeoning new field for the firm.*

Left: *110 leaflet.*

More of a Good Thing: The 20 Series

In 1965, a new world design for the smaller tractors in the line was announced to be built in Dubuque and later in Mannheim: The 20 Series initially had two models in the United States, the 1020 and 2020, while in Europe the smaller farms needed five models to satisfy demand, including the 820 (subsequently exported to the United States), 920, and 1120. They followed their larger siblings with front-mounted fuel tanks, gas and diesel engines, eight-speed collar-shift transmissions, and closed-center hydraulics. Add to this their lower-link draft sensing and differential lock, and they proved the match of the larger models.

Late in 1965, a smaller row-crop model was introduced by Waterloo, the 2510, updated in 1969 as the 2520. In 1968, Dubuque added the 1520 to the U.S. line, the equivalent of Mannheim's 1120, while the German works in turn added the 2120 to the European line and the following year, their first six-cylinder model, the 3120. Canada had opted for the Mannheim models starting with the 710.

The need for further refinements for 1964 arrived in the shape of the 3020 and 4020 tractors with Power Shift transmission options and hydraulic differential locks. These machines led the way for the 5020 to follow in 1965.

Also in 1968, Deere's first turbocharged tractor, the 122-hp 4520—an enlarged 4020—joined the lengthening line; it in turn was replaced late in 1970 with the 4620, now intercooled as well as turbocharged.

Meanwhile, the 8010 was updated in 1963 to the 8020. While waiting for the next Waterloo design of articulated four-wheel-drive models, an arrangement was made with the Wagner Tractor Company of Portland, Oregon, to market its WA-14 and WA-17 models, suitably restyled to match the others in the Deere line. The Waterloo-designed 7020 duly appeared in 1970, using the same engine as the new 4620. A turbocharged version of the 4020, the 4320, was announced at the same time.

The new 4020 with Roll-Gard.

A 2020 with cutting blade.

Above and left: *A restored 4020 Hi-Crop. (Photographs by Chester Peterson Jr.)*

More of a Good Thing: The 20 Series

A lineup of 20 Series machines. (Photograph by Chester Peterson Jr.)

Over-all height is 65 inches.
Over-all width is 77-5/8 inches.

No-hang-up shielding protects you and your trees.

A cast-iron-and-steel "nose" guards the front of the 2020.

Large tires provide good flotation.

Engine compartment screens may be removed easily for engine servicing.

Swept-back front axle and power steering give you excellent maneuverability.

2020 Orchard brochure.

*A 920 tills
spring soil.*

A big 5020 Diesel turns over spring soil.

New 1020 47hp.
TRACTOR

JOHN DEERE

JOHN DEERE 1020

Deere's Worldwide Tractor Design Program

By Harold L. Brock

With the introduction of the New Generation tractor Models 3010 and 4010, the rest of Deere's family of tractors needed to be updated. New sheet metal and features were applied to both the smaller and larger series of tractors to identify them as a family of products. The large Model 5010 was introduced with styling and operating features similar to the 4010. A smaller series of tractors were being produced by Deere's Dubuque factory and an entirely different series of tractors by the Mannheim works. The Dubuque factory 1010 and 2010 Series competed in the popular utility market with leaders such as Ford and Massey-Harris-Ferguson. The Mannheim series of tractors were Europe's New Generation designs with Dubuque engines and Mannheim transmissions. Both the Dubuque and Mannheim series of tractors differed in basic design concept and features from those in the 3010 and 4010 New Generation tractors. Dealer and customer preference for the Waterloo tractor concept of design brought pressure on Deere management to develop a worldwide concept that would bring the total family of tractors into agreement in component design. Engine type and powertrains plus hydraulic controls would provide uniformity throughout the line of products. This would offer both marketing and manufacturing advantages.

Deere management asked me to chair a committee to establish the parameters of such a program. A committee was formed with representatives from worldwide marketing, engineering, and manufacturing. The program was defined to design and develop two sizes of tractors to replace the Dubuque and Mannheim series. Marketing objectives were established to meet head on the competition from Ford and Massey-Harris-Ferguson. I relished this challenge as it permitted me to improve upon the basic Ford designs I had developed in the 9N, 2N, and 8N series. Inasmuch as the Massey-Harris-Ferguson tractors were a copy of the Ford design, this simplified the planning process.

Chief engineers from Dubuque, Germany, and France worked with Deere Waterloo product engineering. They played an important part in establishing functional characteristics to be incorporated in the program and meet worldwide requirements. As the product would be produced in many areas of the world, manufacturing considerations were key, but this also raised interesting, unforeseen dilemmas.

At that point in time, industry product drawings were dimensioned in inch decimals. When products were produced overseas new drawings had to be made with metric conversions and rounding off the numerical equivalent. In precision measurements, this created confusion and a possible misfit of parts. And the U.S. drawings used a different projection system than metric countries: A part made from a U.S. drawing would be the opposite hand of the metric counterpart. Further, when drawings were redrawn, notes had to be transcribed in the local language. And finally, U.S. material gauges and chemical content in many cases were not available in many foreign countries.

After much discussion and compromise, the engineers agreed that the worldwide drawings should reflect the U.S. projection. The American engineers agreed that the drawings would be dimensioned in the even metric numbers, although both metric and inch dimensions would be shown. Symbology would be developed to replace printed words to eliminate conversion of language. This was accomplished to indicate reference items such as squareness, roundness, etc. It was agreed that material selection would

European brochure for the World Tractor, Deere's 1020.

favor worldwide availability. This new worldwide industry approach concept proved to be of great manufacturing benefit and was later adopted throughout the automotive industry.

Having agreed upon the basic parameters such as size and process for the program, detail features and functional characteristics were established. These would meet or beat the competition and bring the units into the family of tractors concept.

A review of the Dubuque and Mannheim series of tractors indicated little commonness of parts and design. Further, the factory cost of the current models was over 25 percent higher than Ford and Massey-Harris-Ferguson's equivalent models. The challenge was to develop a better product and take 25 percent out of the factory cost. A further advantage would be that of reducing the total number of parts necessary to produce the two models. This would improve manufacturing costs and increase the volume of common parts. Adopting common concept of components such as introduced in the New Generation tractors would reduce engineering and manufacturing need to update unlike concepts.

To meet necessary cost reductions, a cost objective for all components was established, feasibility studies and many design concepts were developed and costed from sketches and computer analysis before detail designs were finalized. Suppliers of components were given cost objectives for their products. Manufacturing played a critical role in looking over the shoulder of the designers to assure operational savings would occur.

The program met objectives by reducing factory costs by 25 percent and eliminating a third of the parts required for the series of tractors. Upon completion of design, development, and satisfactory field testing, the 1020 and 2020 Series tractors began production at Dubuque and Mannheim. Common tooling was established between sister factories and a worldwide drawing was the source of information. The tractors had similar features and function as the successful 3020 and 4020 Series of Waterloo tractors.

With the 1020 and 2020 tractors, Deere set a new milestone in its worldwide tractor concept that might never be hailed by tractor enthusiasts. Yet this program positioned Deere & Company to become and maintain its position as the world's leader in tractor and farm machinery manufacture.

Deere employees at work on a 1020 and 2020.

1020 Orchard brochure.

Above and Top: *A restored 2020. (Photograph by Chester Peterson Jr.)*

Deere Harvester Upgrades

Harvester development continued apace with Deere's tractors. The 215 self-propelled windrower was introduced in 1961 and soon overtook the tractor-drawn models in sales. The same year saw the 105 five-straw-walker combine give the company a five-model self-propelled line; its 106 tractor-drawn equivalent also meant a five-model line on that front.

For specialist growers in the American Southwest, Deere introduced the 10 Hi-Density baler in 1963, making 10x15-inch bales and the 323-W three-wire heavy-duty model with 16x23-inch bales up to 50 inches long.

But only limited numbers were made. Another machine with transport in mind was the 400 self-propelled hay cuber introduced in 1965, later becoming the 425 in 1970. Ottumwa also built a stationery 390 model.

Introduced in 1974, Stack Wagons became another type of hay conservation, and the next year Deere introduced its first of many Round Balers.

Cylinder-type forage harvesters replaced flywheel models in 1966. In 1972, Deere introduced its first self-propelled models, the 5200 and 5400.

Above: *Deere's No. 400 hay cuber works a field, 1956.*

Right: *The 4400 New Generation combine, 1968.*

A 4400 combining corn.

A 4400 with grain head and air-conditioned cab.

Life on the Farm in the 1960s and 1970s

Junior takes to the field on his pedal tractor.

Here's a car built to support any population explosion. It's a Ford Country Squire looking young all over.

More brawn in the body puts more life in today's Ford Motor Company cars

Young bodies grow strong with exercise. But a car body has to be born rugged. Especially with a flock of husky youngsters in the family.

How long a life your car body has depends on how solidly it's built. If it's not strong—wear and tear, squeaks and rattles. That's why all Ford-built cars give you so much extra reinforcing.

Take the roof those youngsters are perched on. Three separate steel braces make it super-solid to sit on for ride under! Doors are built like a safe. Steel inside and out. That means stronger, safer, quieter doors. Slam one—you can tell by the sound they're solidly built. Underneath, too, extra heavy construction keeps the body more solid and silent.

even over twisting, washboard roads. Engineering excellence like this puts more value into Ford Motor Company cars wherever you look. It's all part of a plan to give you today's best-built cars. A plan where engineering designs the quality for the car. Manufacturing precision puts it there. Severe testing sees that it stays there.

RIDE WALT DISNEY'S MAGIC SKYWAY AT THE FORD MOTOR COMPANY WONDER ROTUNDA, NEW YORK WORLD'S FAIR

Ford-built means better built *Ford* MUSTANG•FALCON•FAIRLANE•FORD•THUNDERBIRD
COMET•MERCURY•LINCOLN CONTINENTAL
MOTOR COMPANY

Deere's Generation II Tractors

For Deere, 1972 was to be another key year. The entire board of directors met for the first time in Europe, and Saarbrücken, Germany, was chosen as the venue for the announcement in August of the new Generation II tractors. Thousands of dealers gathered in a large auditorium with a giant screen showing film with an announcer sitting in the cab of a tractor. He detailed all the features of this new unit, then opened the cab door—to an audible gasp from the audience! The tractor's engine had been running during the whole presentation, and no one had realized it. The new Sound-Gard body, as it was known, became the cab by which all future cabs were judged.

The four new models were the 80-hp 4030, 100-hp 4230 (the replacement for the classic 4020), 125-hp turbocharged 4430, and the 150-hp turbocharged and intercooled 4630. The first 30 Series tractor had been the 2030, the last Deere tractor tested at Nebraska with a gas engine, replacing the 2020 the previous year. The 2030 was followed in 1972 by the 6030 replacing the 5020, which was unique in being offered with the choice of two engines: the 141-hp of the 5020, or the 175-hp used in the 7520, another 1972 announcement.

It was 1974 before the 7020 and 7520 were replaced with the 175-hp 8430 and 225-hp 8630 with 30 Series styling and Sound-Gard cab. In the United States, the other two smaller, 830 and 2630 models joined the 30 Series in 1972, but with the "old" styling. In Europe, too, the 1630 through 3130 line was announced that year, but the four smaller machines remained as the 20 Series. It was 1975 before all models were given the later, round-nose style. Starting with the 3130 in 1974, a new Operators Protection Unit (OPU) was introduced in Europe, and gradually was applied to all models down to the 1030.

A 6030 Diesel prepares for spring planting.

A 2030 fitted with a Roll-Gard canopy and cutting blade.

A new slope-nose 4435 with 3751 disk plow, 1974.

A 4630 with 110 Cult-Planter and 220 sprayer, 1972.

Enter Generation II
New Sound-Idea Tractors
from John Deere

In 1960, John Deere's New Generation of Power burst into being, making obsolete many other concepts of modern tractor design. Now Generation II explodes into action applying sound engineering technology to performance, reliability, features, and human engineering, including control of sound itself...the new Sound-Idea tractors.

Generation II brochure.

A 4630 with a 350 disk, 1975.

The Launch of the 40 Series

In 1975, the four smaller models changed to the 40 Series, still with the rear-sloping hood. The 2040 and 2240 were built in Mannheim; the 2440 and 2640 in Dubuque. A six-cylinder 2840 from Mannheim was added in 1976, the equivalent of the European 3130.

The Waterloo two-wheel-drive tractors were updated to the 40 Series in 1978 as the new Iron Horses, followed by the 8440 and 8640 the next year. The last twin-front-wheel models were of the 40 Series, which also saw the introduction of a fifth model, the 180-PTO-hp 4840.

With the introduction of the 40 Series in Europe in 1979, the decision was made to equip these models with the Sound-Gard II cab to be built in the new works in Bruchsal, Germany. An additional model in this series, the 3640, with mechanical front-wheel drive (MFWD) as standard, was added in 1984; it was Deere's first tractor so equipped. It also meant the rear upswept hood style, like the larger models, was adopted; again, the six-cylinder 2940 in the United States was the first to be so equipped. It enabled the U.S. models to be introduced as "The New Profiles of Performance."

A 2140 fitted with canopy.

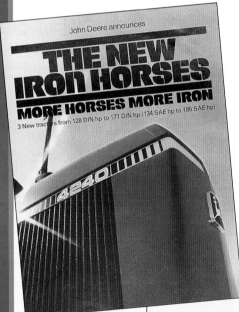

"The New Iron Horses" 40 Series brochure.

A 4440 pulls a 1508 mower.

A 2240 Orchard at work, 1979.

A 8640 four-wheel drive.

The Debut of the 50 Series

Late in 1977 for the 1978 season, a 50 Series of under-40-hp three-cylinder tractors with Deere engines, built in Japan by Yanmar, was announced. The first two models, the 850 and 950, were subsequently joined over eight years by seven more models: the 650 and 750, a specialist 25-hp 900 HC, and four larger machines, the 1050 through 1650. The 1450 and 1650 were four-cylinder tractors with 50- and 60-hp engines respectively. The 1650 broke several records when tested at Nebraska.

In late 1982, Deere's agricultural tractor factories introduced ten new two-wheel-drive 50 Series models—five from Mannheim in the 2150 through 2950 machines, and five from Waterloo in the 4050 through 4850—as well as three four-wheel-drives, 8450, 8650, and 8850. The 8850 was the firm's first V-8 tractor model and its largest to date, boasting 300 PTO hp. All two-wheel-drive models had the option of Caster/Action MFWD. The European models were sold in the United States as New Efficiency Experts, while the Waterloo models had a fifteen-speed Power Shift option, standard on the 4850. Initially both the 4050 and 4250 were offered as Hi-Crop models, but the former was soon dropped as demand was for the more powerful machine. In 1985, an extra model, the 95-hp 3150, was announced from Mannheim, again with MFWD standard.

A 2750 Orchard weaves through trees.

A Yanmar-built 750, 1981.

A 4850 disks corn stubble.

An 8650 harvests corn.

The Upgraded 55 Series

For the sesquicentennial anniversary of the company, the Mannheim models were upgraded to the 55 Series. With a choice of five transmissions and speciality models—two orchard/vineyard, two High Clearance (Mudders), and four wide-tracks—the line was extensive.

At Palm Springs, California, in January 1989, the Waterloo tractors followed suit, with an extra-wide-frame model, the 155-hp 4555, added. The four-wheel-drive models, from 200- to 322-PTO-hp, had been completely redesigned the previous fall and became the 60 Series. Completely new styling, with the muffler and air intake moved to the right-hand corner of the new-style cab to give a clear front view, three new transmissions, and a longer-wheelbase chassis with center-frame oscillation all gave them a modern look.

An under-40-hp 55 Series of hydrostatic-drive compact tractors was announced in 1986. The line initially featured just three models—the 655, 755, and 855—followed in 1989 with the 955 and in 1993 with the 455. For customers who preferred gear-driven models, another series was introduced in 1989, the 670 through 1070. Also built by Yanmar, they replaced the earlier 50 Series.

Above: *A 655 at work tending a lawn.*

Left: *A Yanmar-built 955, 1989.*

A 2955 Wide Track with Roll-Gard prepares soil.

A 2255 Orchard, 1986.

Robert A. Hanson became Deere & Company president, chairman, and CEO in 1982. He served until 1990.

Combines and Balers New Generations

For 1970, the New Generation of four basic models of combines had completely new features including an integrated cab as standard, the engine moved ahead of the grain tank and alongside the cab, and augers used to convey the grain from below the walkers to the sieve area. Variations of the basic models were built for corn, rice (R), and hillside (H) use. A decade later, the Titan 20 Series range for 1979 dropped the 3300 and added a new six-walker 8820 at the top of the range.

The year 1989 saw the introduction of the three Maxi-mizer model combines in the United States, reverting to the original central cab position and engine behind the tank, a layout retained by Zweibrücken, Germany, for European models.

The smallest U.S. combine, the 4400 was updated to the 4420 in 1980 and then replaced by the 4425 from Europe in 1986; it in turn became the 4435 in 1989. In Europe, the 900 Series of 1972–1976, the 925 through 985 Series of 1976–1981, and the eight-model 1000 Series of 1982–1992 all retained the classic 55 layout.

CORN AND BEAN COMBINES

Titan II Series combine brochure, 1987.

A pulled 7721 combine, 1978.

A SideHill 6600 combine, 1975.

Left: *20 Series combine brochure, 1979.*

Below: *A Turbo 7700 combine at work, 1978.*

CHAPTER 6

The World's Leader, 1991–2003

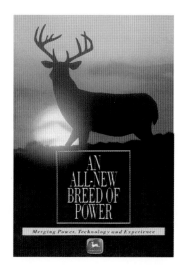

The modern Deere at work: A 9300T prepares a field.

Introducing the Thousand Series

When Deere & Company takes a giant step forward in its tractor design, it leaves the competition in its wake. In 1960, it was the New Generation. In 1972, it was the Generation II Sound-Gard Body. And in 1991, it was the introduction of the Thousand Series.

The first of the new Thousand Series was the 5000 models, which were built in a new factory in Augusta, Georgia. Initially, a trio of three-cylinder models was announced—the 40-hp 5200, 50-hp 5300, and 60-hp 5400—followed in 1992 by a narrow version of the largest, the 5400N for vineyard and orchard work. In 1995, the line was expanded with the four-cylinder 70-hp 5500 and 5500N; in 1996, cabs were available for both the standard and narrow models.

For 1998, the line was updated to the 5000 Ten Series, with the two smaller machines having Model 3029 three-cylinder engines; the two larger, 4045 four-cylinders; and the 5510 being turbocharged. All the new models boasted a 5-hp increase in power.

In Europe, the 5000 Series was introduced in 1996 and built in Italy, and upgraded to the 5010 Series in 2000. In the United States, it became the 5000 Twenty Series in 2000. That same year, the 5010 Series was also built in a new factory in Punc, India.

For two years, 1991 and 1992, the larger wide-framed Waterloo tractors were upgraded to the 60 Series for the U.S. market, although they remained the 55 Series in Europe.

Both Mannheim and Waterloo introduced their four-cylinder 6000 and six-cylinder 7000 Series in 1992 as "An All New Breed of Power," with a new modular design in an independent steel main frame, plus completely new cabs with two-door access, called ComfortGard in the United States and TechCenter in Europe. Open-station with two-post foldable ROPS and two- or four-wheel drive were optional on all models.

Additions to the 6000 Series were introduced in Europe: two six-cylinder models in 1993, the 6600 and 6800, with the 6900 added the next year and the 6506 in 1995. Economy SE models in Europe and Advantage in the States were added in 1996 and 1997 respectively, and the whole line was changed to the 6000 Ten Series in 1998.

The 6000 Twenty Series was introduced at Albuquerque, New Mexico, in the United States and the 6020 Series in Seville, Spain, in fall 2001, as part of the company's largest new product announcements ever, with more than sixty new machines. The tractors featured new styling, tilt hoods, new transmissions, and other new options. For 2003, four economy models were announced in August 2002: the 6000 Fifteen Series including the four-cylinder 72-hp 6215 and 85-hp 6415, and six-cylinder 95-hp 6615 and 105-hp 6715. All four models were available with cab or open station.

The original three 7000 Series saw two models added in 1993, the 7200 and 7400, with Hi-Crop and High Clearance versions also available. The whole 7000 Series became the 7000 Ten Series in 1996. In 1997, the 7405 Advantage economy model was added. A sixth size, the 7510, was added in 2000.

Also announced for the U.S. market in August 2002 was the four-model 7000 Twenty Series in the narrow-frame size, including the 95-hp 7220, 105-hp 7320, 115-hp 7420, and 125-hp 7520. Available with cab or open station, and with a new Infinitely Variable Transmission (IVT) available as an option, with three other PowrQuad options. They were designed in Mannheim but built in Waterloo.

For 2003, two economy models, the 30-hp 790 and 40-hp 990 were announced with Yanmar engines and optional MFWD, and a new 2000 Series Compact Utility Tractor, the 23-hp 2210 4WD model.

Also for 2003, a new three-model 5020 Series was introduced from Mannheim, including the 72-hp 5620, 80-hp 5720, and 88-hp 5820. They replaced the four-model Renault 3010 series for Europe, and are really smaller versions of the 6020 Series with a full-frame design and Deere PowerTech four-cylinder engines. Initially, they were only MFWD with either sixteen-speed PowerQuad or PowerQuad Plus transmissions. They fill a significant gap in the Long Green Line of Tractors from the 18-hp 4010 to the 450-hp 9520.

This leaves only the three large-frame 7000 Ten Series from Waterloo to receive the Twenty Series treatment given the rest of the line.

Why it pays to use John Deere money for your equipment needs

John Deere Finance Plans
Designed specially for your equipment needs

Above: *The compact 4700 tractor with cab.*

Right: *A 5000 Ten Series brochure.*

A 5510 hauls haybales.

Introducing the Thousand Series

6000 Series brochure, 1996.

6200–6400 brochure, 1992.

7010 Series European brochure.

A 6910 S tractor.

A 7810 mounted with a rear 1365 mower-conditioner and group and front 228A mower-conditioner.

A 6410 MFWD plows a field for spring planting.

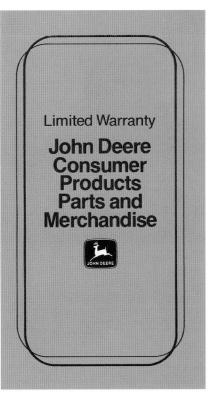

Deere's new 5020 Series was launched in 2003, featuring the 88-hp 5820.

A COMPLETE RANGE OF LUBRICANTS, **FOR ALL-ROUND PROTECTION.**

JOHN DEERE
RELIABILITY IS OUR STRENGTH

Above: *Deere lubricants brochure.*

Left: *Deere's 2003 7520.*

The Big Boys: The 8000 and 9000 Series

The largest two-wheel-drive models ever built by Deere were introduced in 1994 with four models from the 160-PTO-hp 8100 to the 225-hp 8400. A rubber-tracked version of all four, the 8000T Series was announced in 1997. All eight models were updated to the 8000 Ten Series in 2000, in turn becoming the 8000 Twenty Series in fall 2001 with a fifth new model, the 295-hp 8520 and 8520T added. The new models offered more power, 250- to 295-engine-hp, more lift capacity, and greater comfort, with Independent Link Suspension (ILS) front axle as an option for the wheeled models and ActiveSeat Suspension (ASS) for all.

Larger still were the four 9000 Series articulated four-wheel-drive models announced in 1996. Their tracked versions arrived in 1999. The 9000 bypassed the Ten Series to go straight to the 9000 Twenty Series in 2001 at the same time as the other series.

At the other end of the scale, the under-50-hp, Augusta-built 4000 Series started in 1997 with the 20-engine-hp 4100. It was joined in 1998 by five other models, from the 263-hp 4200 to the 43-hp 4600, and a sixth in 2000, the 47-hp 4700. For 2002, they became the 4000 Ten Series with two additional models, the 18-gross-hp 4010 and 25-hp 4115. The 4010, 21-hp 4110, 4115, 28-hp 4210, 32-hp 4310, and 35-hp 4410 had three-cylinder engines; the 39-hp 4510, 44-hp 4610, and 48-hp 4710 had four-cylinders.

For 2003, two economy models—the 30-engine-hp 790 and 40-hp 990—were announced, with Yanmar engines and optional MFWD.

It's not the similarities that upset our competitors . . .

NEW 136 to 191 kW (185 to 260 hp) John Deere 8000T Series Tractors

Above: *An 8300 discs a field.*

Left: *8000T leaflet.*

8000/8000T SERIES
160- TO 225-HP TRACTORS ON TIRES OR TRACKS

JOHN DEERE INTRODUCES

THE NEW THOROUGHBREDS OF POWER

21st CENTURY TECHNOLOGY TODAY

Above: *8000/8000T Series brochure.*

Right: *8000 Series brochure.*

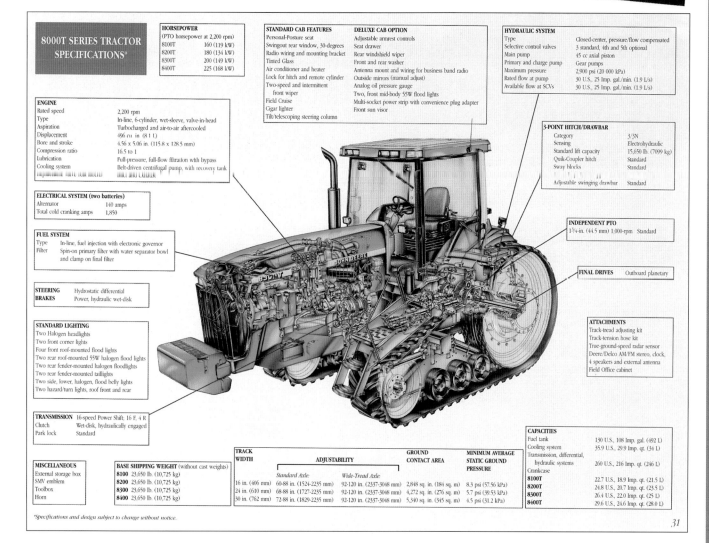

8000T SERIES TRACTOR SPECIFICATIONS*

HORSEPOWER
(PTO horsepower at 2,200 rpm)

8100T	160 (119 kW)
8200T	180 (134 kW)
8300T	200 (149 kW)
8400T	225 (168 kW)

ENGINE

Rated speed	2,200 rpm
Type	In-line, 6-cylinder, wet-sleeve, valve-in-head
Aspiration	Turbocharged and air-to-air aftercooled
Displacement	496 cu. in. (8.1 L)
Bore and stroke	4.56 x 5.06 in. (115.8 x 128.5 mm)
Compression ratio	16.5 to 1
Lubrication	Full-pressure, full-flow filtration with bypass
Cooling system	Belt-driven centrifugal pump, with recovery tank

ELECTRICAL SYSTEM (two batteries)

Alternator	140 amps
Total cold cranking amps	1,850

FUEL SYSTEM

Type	In-line, fuel injection with electronic governor
Filter	Spin-on primary filter with water separator bowl and clamp on final filter

STEERING Hydrostatic differential
BRAKES Power, hydraulic wet-disk

STANDARD LIGHTING
Two Halogen headlights
Two front corner lights
Four front roof-mounted flood lights
Two rear roof-mounted 55W halogen flood lights
Two rear fender-mounted halogen floodlights
Two rear fender-mounted taillights
Two side, lower, halogen, flood belly lights
Two hazard/turn lights, roof front and rear

TRANSMISSION 16-speed Power Shift; 16 F, 4 R
Clutch Wet-disk, hydraulically engaged
Park lock Standard

MISCELLANEOUS
External storage box
SMV emblem
Toolbox
Horn

STANDARD CAB FEATURES
Personal-Posture seat
Swingout rear window, 30-degrees
Radio wiring and mounting bracket
Tinted Glass
Air conditioner and heater
Lock for hitch and remote cylinder
Two-speed and intermittent front wiper
Field Cruise
Cigar lighter
Tilt/telescoping steering column

DELUXE CAB OPTION
Adjustable armrest controls
Seat drawer
Rear windshield wiper
Front and rear washer
Antenna mount and wiring for business band radio
Outside mirrors (manual adjust)
Analog oil pressure gauge
Two, front mid-body 55W flood lights
Multi-socket power strip with convenience plug adapter
Front sun visor

HYDRAULIC SYSTEM

Type	Closed-center, pressure/flow compensated
Selective control valves	3 standard, 4th and 5th optional
Main pump	45 cc axial piston
Primary and charge pump	Gear pumps
Maximum pressure	2,900 psi (20 000 kPa)
Rated flow at pump	30 U.S., 25 Imp. gal./min. (1.9 L/s)
Available flow at SCVs	30 U.S., 25 Imp. gal./min. (1.9 L/s)

3-POINT HITCH/DRAWBAR

Category	3/3N
Sensing	Electrohydraulic
Standard lift capacity	15,650 lb. (7099 kg)
Quik-Coupler hitch	Standard
Sway blocks	Standard
Adjustable swinging drawbar	Standard

INDEPENDENT PTO
1¾-in. (44.5 mm) 1,000-rpm Standard

FINAL DRIVES Outboard planetary

ATTACHMENTS
Track-tread adjusting kit
Track-tension hose kit
True-ground-speed radar sensor
Deere/Delco AM/FM stereo, clock, 4 speakers and external antenna
Field Office cabinet

BASE SHIPPING WEIGHT (without cast weights)	
8100	23,650 lb. (10,725 kg)
8200	23,650 lb. (10,725 kg)
8300	23,650 lb. (10,725 kg)
8400	23,650 lb. (10,725 kg)

TRACK WIDTH	ADJUSTABILITY		GROUND CONTACT AREA	MINIMUM AVERAGE STATIC GROUND PRESSURE
	Standard Axle:	Wide-Tread Axle:		
16 in. (406 mm)	60-88 in. (1524-2235 mm)	92-120 in. (2337-3048 mm)	2,848 sq. in. (184 sq. m)	8.3 psi (57.56 kPa)
24 in. (610 mm)	68-88 in. (1727-2235 mm)	92-120 in. (2337-3048 mm)	4,272 sq. in. (276 sq. m)	5.7 psi (39.53 kPa)
30 in. (762 mm)	72-88 in. (1829-2235 mm)	92-120 in. (2337-3048 mm)	5,340 sq. in. (345 sq. m)	4.5 psi (31.2 kPa)

CAPACITIES

Fuel tank	130 U.S., 108 Imp. gal. (492 L)
Cooling system	35.9 U.S., 29.9 Imp. qt. (34 L)
Transmission, differential, hydraulic systems	260 U.S., 216 Imp. qt. (246 L)
Crankcase	
8100T	22.7 U.S., 18.9 Imp. qt. (21.5 L)
8200T	24.8 U.S., 20.7 Imp. qt. (23.5 L)
8300T	26.4 U.S., 22.0 Imp. qt. (25 L)
8400T	29.6 U.S., 24.6 Imp. qt. (28.0 L)

*Specifications and design subject to change without notice.

31

Details of the 8300T.

The Big Boys: The 8000 and 9000 Series

An 8120 works a field.

8000 brochure, 1994.

9400 advertisement.

8000/8000T
brochure.

SIGN OF THE RIGHT CHOICE

JOHN DEERE

TIRES and TRACKS
STRAIGHT TALK
FROM JOHN DEERE

Above: *The new 9420T upon its unveiling in Spain in 2001.*

Right: *An 8400T.*

Montage of Deere's 2001–2002 lineup with the 8520 wheeled tractor at center.

Deere's Specialist Models

Beginning in 1987, Deere arranged with Goldoni in Italy to produce orchard and vineyard models in the 40- to 70-hp range for small farms in Europe. The line had three models initially, followed by four 45 Series machines built until 1997, when they were replaced with the 46 Series, with three models under 32 hp and three from 45 to 71 hp.

In 1993, in Europe, two other series had been built by outside suppliers: the eight-model 2000 Series built by Zetor in the Czech Republic and sold as a lower-cost line for certain export markets, and the four-model 3000 Series from Renault in France, fitted with Saran-built Deere engines. They were offered in standard, deluxe (X), and economy (SF) versions until 1998, when they were upgraded to the 3010 Series with the same three options.

In 1998, Deere acquired SLC in Brazil, which had been assembling tractors for the Region I market. SLC built seven tractor models from the 75-hp N/A 5600 to the 140-hp turbocharged 7500.

A specialized 3000 Telehandler Series was introduced, first in Europe from the Zweibrücken works in Germany. Two models—the 3200 and 3400—were launched in 2000, followed by two pivot-steer models in 2002, the 3700 and 3800. The U.S. market had the 3200 and 3400 in 2001 and the 3800 in August 2002.

A 3200 pivot-steer Telehandler with its lift extended.

Above: *Tending the lawn with a 455.*

Left: *A 3800 pivot-steer Telehandler stacks haybales.*

Moving Earth: The Construction Business

Deere first offered an industrial version of its Model D painted in highway yellow back in 1935. Deere entered the construction business in a big way when it started the Industrial Euipment Division in 1958.

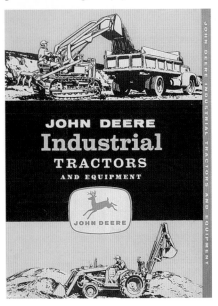

20 Industrial Series brochure.

Above: *An 840 fitted with a Hancock piggyback scraper, 1958.*

820I brochure.

Above: *A JD740 articulated skidder for logging work.*

Left: *A 400G crawler, 1990.*

Right: *A 310C mounted with bulldozer blade and backhoe.*

Below: *A JD570-A motor road grader, 1972.*

A 2355 mounted with a rear box scraper, 1987.

Deere Ventures: From Bicycles to Snowmobiles to NASCAR Racing

Right: *Deere returned to building bicycles in 1974 when its Consumer Products Division imported a full line of models.*

Below: *Deere built a much loved line of snowmobiles at its John Deere Horicon, Wisconsin, Works from 1972 to 1984. Just as Deere tractors are collected, Deere snowmobiles have a fanatical following today.*

NOTHING RUNS LIKE A DEERE

Deere went racing in 1996, sponsoring driver Chad Little in the #23 Pontiac Grand Prix for the NASCAR Busch Grand National Series. In 1997, Deere moved into the NASCAR Winston Cup Series with its #97 Ford Taurus with Little still at the wheel. Deere's race car was retired in mid 2000.

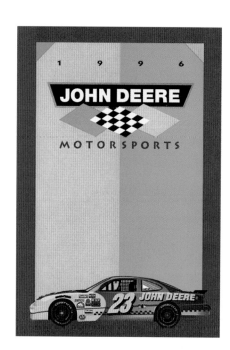

Deere's 1978 Spitfire and Trailfire snowmobiles.

Deere Motorsports schedule for 1990.

The Modern Combine and Harvester Lines

In the United States, the three-model Maximizer combine line was introduced in 1989, and a SideHill version added in 1994. The same year, a CTS model with twin-tine separators in place of straw walkers was introduced, initially for rice. For 1995, it was also introduced for small grain.

A new breed of sprayer was introduced in 1996, the 4700, a cross between a Wide-Axle and Hi-Crop tractor, with an integral mounted sprayer, an 8000 Series tractor cab, six-cylinder 6.8-liter 185-hp turbocharged engine, four-wheel independent-strut suspension, and three-range hydrostatic transmission. Other sprayers in the line included the general-purpose 6500, while three new self-propelled sprayers were announced the same year: the three-wheel 6100, four-wheel 6600 with optional Mud-Hog front-wheel assist, and the all-new integral hooded sprayer, the 320.

In the mid 1990s, large-capacity balers and windrowers meant the company covered the requirements of commercial hay growers. The announcement of the 100 Big Square baler making 31.5x31.5x98-inch bales, and the 4890 self-propelled windrower with a 4.5-liter 100-hp PowerTech engine were just two of the machines available.

With the advent of the new PowerTech engines, both the standard and CTS combines were updated in 1997, the former to the Ten Series and the latter to the CTS II. The 9510 and 9610 and the CTS had the 8.1-liter engines with 220 or 240 hp on the 9510, and the 275 or 308-hp version on the 9610 and CTS II. The new models also had a new Air Flow feeder house and a new thirteen-bar Generation II concave.

It was in 1997 that Deere took on a joint marketing venture with the Jiamusi Combine Harvester factory in

China to build combines for that vast market. In 1998, Deere acquired Cameco of Thibodaux, Louisiana, with a factory in Catalao, Brazil, where it built sugarcane harvesters.

In 1999 the whole U.S. combine line was new, with the introduction of the 50 Series family, including four cylinder-walker separator combines, the 9450, 9550, Sidehill 9550, and 9650 WTS; one cylinder-tine separator machine, the 9650 CTS; and two single-tine separator models, the 9650 and 9750 STS.

Experiments were conducted in Europe in 1998 with the U.S.-built CTS combine, and it was offered with a 305-hp engine for 1999. But farmers had to wait until 2001 for the 9000 Series. These Zweibrücken-built combines also had three types of separators, the new six-model Walker-Tine Separator (WTS) machines with a powered-tine separator to comb the straw as it passed over the walkers, and the CTS and STS machines like the U.S. models. In addition a lower-priced Cylinder-Walker Series (CWS) was built in Brazil, with two models, the 1450-CWS and 1550-CWS. All four series had the central cab and engine-behind-tank layout, which has always been a feature of the extra-straw-requirement models in Europe.

The six WTS models were the five-walker 9540, 9560, and 9580, and six-walker 9640, 9660, and 9680. The 9780 CTS model had the same 310-hp engine as the 9680 WTS model, while the 9880 STS was marketed as the world's largest-capacity combine with a 430-hp engine, and it shared the largest 11,000-liter grain tank with the 9680 WTS.

With the new century, cotton pickers and strippers—earlier models of which had been helping cotton pickers for more than fifty years—were updated. The six-row 7455 Stripper and the world's first production six-row picker, the 9976, were introduced.

From Arc-les-Gray in France, the European equivalent of Ottumwa in the United States, came all the grass machinery, including the new front-mounted, rear-mounted, side-pull, and center-pivot Mo-Cos, fixed- and variable-chamber round balers, and an all-new 678 Wrapping Baler.

In fall 2002, four new 7000 Series self-propelled forage harvesters were announced: the 315-hp 7200, 415-hp 7300, 500-hp 7400, and the 570-hp 7500.

From Horst in the Netherlands, a complete line of mounted and tractor-drawn sprayers was added to the already full line of machinery on offer. When the U.S. sprayers were updated in 2000, both the 200-hp 4710 and 106-hp 6700, replacements for the 4700 and 6600, were built in the Comeco works in Louisiana.

A 1158 combine powered by a 127-hp engine and featuring 24x41-inch cylinder.

The Modern Combine and Harvester Lines

A 4425 combine harvests corn.

9500 SideHill combine brochure.

A 7720 Titan II combine harvests a rice field.

Deere's 2003 9650 STS combine.

TIMELINE

1991: Deere launches its Thousand Series tractors built in a new factory in Augusta, Georgia. The Soviet Union dissolves after a failed coup attempt, officially ending the Cold War. Persian Gulf War is fought. South Africa repeals Apartheid Laws. Farmers make up 2.6 percent of the U.S. labor force with farms averaging 461 acres.

1992: Deere's Mannheim and Waterloo works introduce their four-cylinder 6000 and six-cylinder 7000 Series as "An All New Breed of Power."

1994: Channel Tunnel opens, connecting Britain and France.

1996: Mad Cow Disease hits Britain.

1997: Deere launches its flagship crawler 8000T Series, followed by the 9000T.1999. Princess Diana Dies in car crash.

1998: Deere marks 75 years of building tractors. Congress threatens to impeach U.S. President Bill Clinton. Viagra debuts.

2000: Dawn of the new millenium. Robert W. Lane is elected chairman of Deere's board of directors.

2001: Terrorists crash hijacked planes into the World Trade Center and Pentagon.

2003: Deere builds tractors for the world market with factories in North America, South America, South Africa, Europe, and elsewhere around the globe.

Deere's Pocket Ledgers: A Restrospective

Deere & Company issued annual complimentary pocket notebooks to their customers. Along with a calendar and a summary of Deere's equipment offerings, these ledgers were invaluable notebooks for keeping tallies of expenditures, stock and crop records, and important dates.

An 1896, thirtieth annual edition.

Above: The 1906 Farmers Pocket Companion.

Top: A 1904 ledger from Deere & Webber Company.

Deere's Magazines: A Restrospective

Deere & Company has long published magazines for its employees, dealers, and customers. *John Deere Journal* is Deere's employee publication. Deere also publishes other magazines for collectors, home owners, and various ag and construction specialties.

Yet *The Furrow* is the firm's most famous magazine dating back to spring 1895. As of 2003, Deere publishes nine regional editions of *The Furrow* in the United States and three editions in Canada. *The Furrow* is published in eleven languages and circulated in more than forty-five countries with a total worldwide circulation of more than 1.5 million copies.

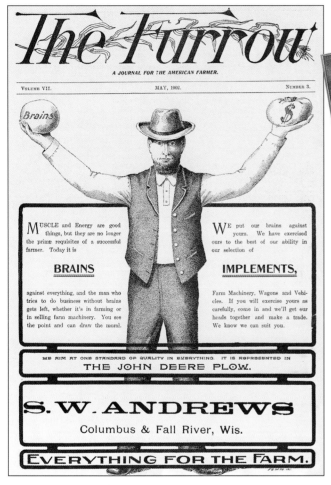

Above: *The May 1902 issue of* The Furrow *promoting the importance of smarts in farming.*

A bicentennial issue of The Furrow from 1975.

The fiftieth anniversary issue featured a farmer reading the first issue from spring 1895.

The Changing Face of Farms Chores

Wash day meant hard work from sun up to sundown, as these two 1920s women show.

Above: *The farmer's daughter, as depicted in a Currier & Ives engraving from the 1860s, holding the wheat she had cut.*

Right: *A milkmaid and Bossie in a calendar print from the 1930s.*

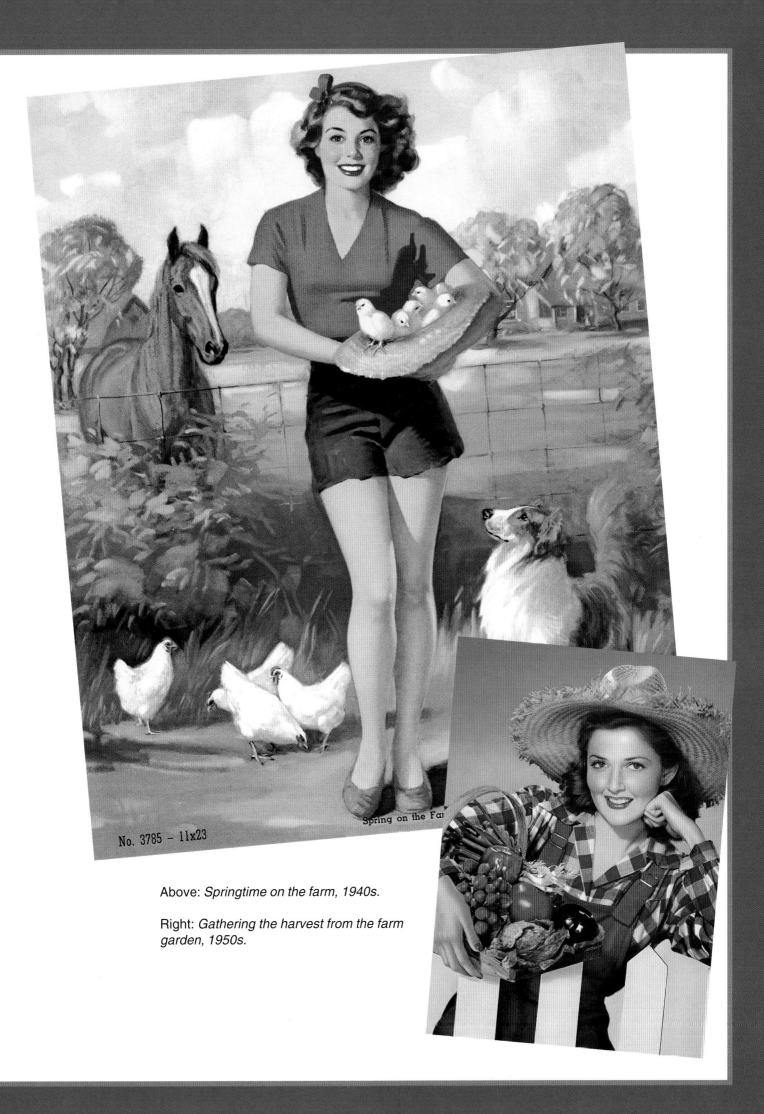

No. 3785 – 11x23

Spring on the Fa[r]

Above: *Springtime on the farm, 1940s.*

Right: *Gathering the harvest from the farm garden, 1950s.*

The Art of Spreading Manure

SO JOHN DEERE NOW OFFERS YOU OVER 2,500 DIFFERENT MANURE-HANDLING COMBINATIONS— TO LET YOU MATCH YOUR SPECIFIC CLEANUP REQUIREMENTS

New **JOHN DEERE** SPREADER

The Low-Down Spreader with the Beater on the Axle and the Box-Roll Turn

JOHN DEERE SPREADER
The Spreader with the Beater on the Axle

MARSEILLES CO. EAST MOLINE, ILL.

THE MANURE SPREADER IS A BOON TO FARMER AND DEALER ALIKE.

The manure spreader was an invention saluted by farmers.

Why This Spreader Will Be One of the Best Investments You Ever Made

Machine spreading showed a $122 average gain over hand spreading on 6 acres of corn and 10 of meadow—per year, in a 3-year experiment.

It showed a gain of $180 on 40 acres of corn as compared to 40 acres unmanured—for one Nebraska farmer.

It encourages hauling more manure—many farmers report hauling 50% more than by hand method.

The New John Deere shreds the manure and spreads it evenly, not in lumps—doubling and tripling the fertilizing power of manure.

"The New John Deere pays its cost back every year"—say many farmers.

"Offers the only way to get a hired man to evenly distribute manure", says one farmer.

"Makes better use of high-priced labor", says another.

Helps boost land values.

Helps save the liquids—the most valuable part of manure—because of the tight bottom and endgate attachment (the latter furnished as an extra).

It is built so low—so easy to load—that you can take time to spread manure fresh from the gutter—daily—preventing losses from heating and leaching, and thus getting the full $4.71 per ton value as outlined in Ohio Bulletin No. XIII—32.

"Brings the biggest returns in the shortest time", says one user.

"The New John Deere has more than doubled our hay crop", says another farmer.

This spreader makes 100 loads go as far as 150 loads spread by hand.

The New John Deere pulverizes the manure unusually well, so that the manure will be better mixed with the soil, keeping the soil loose and warm, more retentive of moisture, more productive and less apt to wash and bake.

It showed a gain over hand spreading of $4.80 per acre in corn, $3.92 per acre in oats and $2.00 per acre in clover—in one Indiana experiment.

It allows one man, one team (or tractor) to do as much as four men and two teams —and do the work better than by hand spreading.

It is built strong for use with a tractor; can be equipped with a tractor hitch and levers; is a valuable unit in any system of tractor farming.

It is a double-purpose machine when equipped with the lime spreading attachment shown on page 11.

It pays an excellent profit on the investment even when there are only 50 loads a year to spread.

It is very durably constructed, giving many years of low-cost service. Mounting the beater on the axle permits simpler construction—fewer parts to wear. High-carbon beater shafts and axles are used, and axles are oversize. The deep box forms a truss with the frame.

Exceptional quality and durability have always characterized John Deere Spreaders. The farmers' average yearly repair bill for the first 150,000 machines was less than 85 cents per machine. Included in these are spreaders having hauled 4,000 to 5,000 or more loads, and being still in daily, satisfactory service.

NEW **JOHN DEERE** MOLINE, ILL. U.S.A.

The **NEW JOHN DEERE** THE SPREADER WITH THE BEATER ON THE AXLE AND THE BOX-ROLL TURN

Deere's Calendars:
Keeping Track of Time Through the Years

Above: *A painting from a 1927 Deere calendar.*

Below: *Deere's 1994 calendar, "Generations of Progress."*

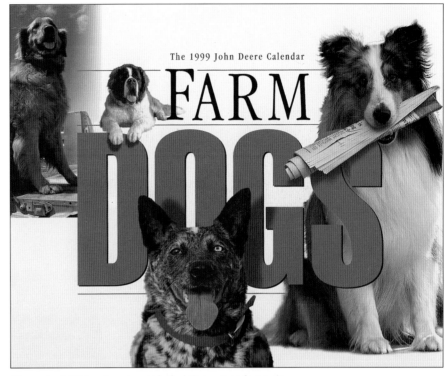

Deere's 1999 calendar saluted the great farm dog.

A 1963 Deere calendar.　　　*A 1954 Deere calendar.*

A 1950s Deere calendar painting by Walter Haskell Hinton.

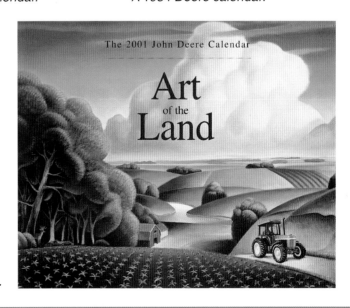

Farm Living Through the Years

A quaint 1860s farm scene from a Currier & Ives engraving.

Above: *Home, sweet sod home: Life on the prairies at the dawn of the 1900s.*

Right: *An idealized farm scene, 1920s.*

Left: *Harvesting corn at the turn of a new century. (Photograph by Hans Halberstadt)*

Below: *Everyone celebrates spring-time in this image from a 1950s Deere calendar.*

SPRING

The Evolution of the Deere Trademark

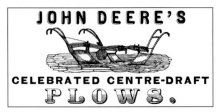

John Deere's woodcut logo from an 1854 advertisement.

Above: *The Deere & Company logo from the firm's 1855 stationary.*

Right: *Deere's 1880 logo.*

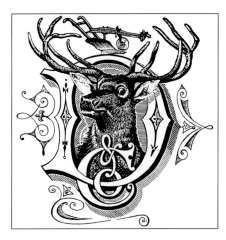

Above: *The Waterloo Gasoline Engine Company's Waterloo Boy logo from 1913.*

Right: *Deere registered its second trademark in 1912, as seen here on the Dain All-Wheel-Drive. The logo was much like the 1876 image but there was more detail drawn into the animal.*

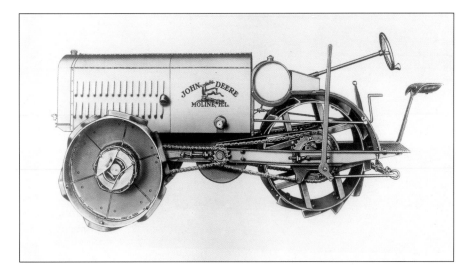

Above: *Lanz's 1930 trademark.*

Above right: *Just one year after the 1936 trademark debuted, a new logo was introduced in 1937 marking Deere's centennial.*

Above: *In 1950, the deer's antlers were turned forward, the tail pointed up, and it was no longer shown bounding over a log. A new slogan—"Quality Farm Equipment"—was added.*

Left: *The logo was changed again in 1956 but not actually registered until 1962.*

Above: *The 1885 logo.*

Right: *Deere first registered its trademark with the leaping deer in 1876, although the image was used earlier. This original trademark represented a type of deer common to Africa, and only in future trademarks was the North American white-tailed deer portrayed.*

Above: *Through the 1920s the logo gradually evolved into the image shown here above the Syracuse Plow Works.*

Left: *Deere's standardization committee sought to "better adapt the trademark for stenciling on products," and a new logo was registered in 1936. The deer became a solid silhouette, provided a stronger, more recognizable profile as Deere was aggressively trying to dominate the tractor market. An angular border was added around the leaping deer. The antlers were changed slightly and the company's name was made bolder. The slogan below read "The Trade Mark of Quality Made Famous by Good Implements."*

Left: *A Deere memo described the 1968 logo update: "The new trademark is in keeping with the progress being made throughout all divisions of the Company . . . it provides for better reproduction and greater readability under a wider range of usage." The design was modernized with a side silhouette with just two legs and one four-point rack of antlers.*

Right: *In 2000, Deere created its latest logo reflecting the strong, positive associations inherent in the revered John Deere name and symbol. The leaping deer now appears to be pushing upward rather than heading toward a landing position. As Deere's website noted, "The style and shape of this updated logo is reflective of today's technology world: bolder, stronger, high technology oriented. In the symbol itself, the deer's feet are rooted firmly into the ground for a strong leap into the new millennium. The body, head and antlers have a purposeful attitude, a sense of direction and a clear commitment to taking charge by running smart."*